The Example of Shakespeare

By the same author

Poems

Songs of a Goat
a verse drama

Three Plays

America Their America

A Reed in the Tide
a selection of poems

Ozidi
an epic play

Casualties
poems 1966/68

The Example of Shakespeare

JOHN PEPPER CLARK

Northwestern University Press, Evanston, 1970

© J. P. Clark 1970

Library of Congress Catalog Card Number 74–135535

ISBN cloth 0–8101–0340–0
ISBN paper 0–8101–0341–9

Printed in Great Britain

PR
9798
C6

Contents

Contents

Acknowledgements

We are grateful to the following for permission to reproduce copyright material:

Frank Cass & Co. Ltd for an extract from *Peoples of Southern Nigeria* by P. A. Talbot; author's agents for an extract from *Mister Johnson* by Joyce Cary; William Heinemann Ltd and Astor-Honor Inc., for an extract from *No Longer at Ease* by Chinua Achebe, Copyright © Chinua Achebe 1960; Indiana University Press for 'I love the days of long ago' by Michael Dei Anang, 'Play Song' by Peter Clark, and 'Blue black' and 'Black blue' by Bloke Modisane all from *Poems from Black Africa* edited by Langston Hughes; International African Institute for an extract from 'The Kalabari Ekine Society: A Borderland of Religion and Art' by Professor R. Horton from *Africa* Vol. 33, No. 2, April 1963; Mr Pius Okigbo for extracts from *Heavensgate*, *Limits* and *Transition No. 18* by Christopher Okigbo; Penguin Books Ltd for extracts from 'Homecoming' by Lenrie Peters, 'Telephone Conversation' by Wole Soyinka, 'Requiem' by Wole Soyinka, and 'Come Away My Love' by Kariuki all from *Modern Poetry from Africa*.

We have been unable to trace the copyright holders of 'Blackman Trouble' and 'Thoughts at Victoria Beach' by Dennis Osadebay, 'Exile in Nigeria' by Ezekiel Mphahlele and 'Sirens, Knuckles and Boots' by Dennis Brutus, and would appreciate any information that would enable us to do so.

Introduction

All the five essays in this collection were written separately and for different occasions. *Themes of African Poetry of English Expression* was read at the International Conference of Poets held in West Berlin in 1964 as part of the city's festival that year. It was published later in *Transition* volume 4 No. 18. *Aspects of Nigerian Drama* began as brief notes to a talk I gave at an English language workshop, organized for secondary school teachers by the Ford Foundation and the Department of Extra-Mural Studies and Adult Education at the University of Ibadan in 1964. It assumed its present form as a paper read to the English Association at the University of Nigeria, Nsukka in 1966, and later published in *Nigeria* No. 89 the same year. *The Communication Line between Poet and Public* was commissioned by *Présence Africaine* and first published in French in that journal in a special number devoted to the World Festival of Negro Arts held in Dakar in 1966. The English original was published later in *African Forum* volume 3 No. 1. *The Useless Scene in Othello*, a study of plot defect in Shakespeare's *Othello*, is the text of a lecture delivered to the Nigerian English Association at the University of Ife in 1968. In contrast, *The Legacy of Caliban* started as a personal search for the kind of language spoken by African and other 'savage' characters in English literature. Promised later as a paper for the National Identity Conference, held in 1968 at the University of Queensland, Brisbane by the Association of Commonwealth Literature, it ended up eventually on the pages of *Black Orpheus* volume 2 No. 1 of which I am co-editor.

Stretching over a period of four years, none of these essays bears any direct relationship to the other, since I was not pursuing any one preconceived theme or thesis when I wrote them. Still, one major subject emerges out of the selection, that of African literature.

Of this I offer no general or comprehensive look. Rather, I have taken a number of peeps at the subject here and there, and the views so revealed remain mine. That I have made little or no changes in my opinions, many of them expressed several years ago, should not be regarded as a personal indulgence on my part in the art of pulling a line of barbed-wire through a group of defenceless people, as my old friend Ezekiel Mphahlele and others reacted after my Berlin paper. It is just that I still consider the shots well taken and ones worth projecting again as they were then. Sometimes, as in *Aspects of Nigerian Drama*, I have by way of postscript enlarged on details that seem to me of special interest. At other times, a feature, first seen in one picture, may appear again in another exposure in a much stronger light, so that the object of search gets identified better in the process.

All this, I hope, will add to a fuller understanding of the subject, a ware now vended everywhere on the world market. The odd thing however is that while promoters and salesmen of the product seem to be making all the fortune by way of professorial chairs, university fellowships and funds from the foundations, the joint holders of the patent to it are on the whole left with half-empty pockets and grudging fame. Perhaps this is the old lot of the inventor!

The other central idea I personally see running through this selection of essays is that of a workman seeking solutions to a number of problems as and when they arose on the job. And probably the one solution he can claim to have found as others before him is the example of the man everybody calls master in and out of the trade. The example is there for the apprentice to follow in the type of tongues the old man gives his peoples according to their individual character and destiny as in *The Tempest*, and the example is there too for the apprentice to avoid in the kind of structural defect which appears in a play like *Othello* when the master himself nods. Hence the title: *The Example of Shakespeare*.

Lagos 1968   J. P. Clark

The Example of Shakespeare

1: *The Legacy of Caliban*

An introduction to the language spoken by
Africans and other 'natives' in English
literature from Shakespeare to Achebe

Caliban and the African in English literature have a problem
in common. By the African in English literature we mean the
'native' created out of imagination by some Prospero as well
as the 'native' who has become himself a creator of characters
after his own image. Their problem is not the obvious one of
dispossession. Of that Caliban never makes us quite forget in
spite of the revels gathering all round. He enters cursing
Prospero and his attendant spirit Ariel:

> As wicket dew as e'er my mother brush'd
> With raven's feather from unwholesome fen
> Drop on you both! a south-west blow on ye,
> And blister you all over!

He would not be intimidated with talks of punishment by
cramps, side-stiches and pinches from devilish urchins
released by magic at night. Boldly he states his case:

> I must eat my dinner.
> This island's mine, by Sycorax my mother,
> Which thou tak'st from me.

He has been done out of his own not by outright conquest but
through the more withering means of wile and guile:

> When thou camest first,
> Thou strok'dst me, and mad'st much of me: wouldst give me
> Water with berries in't; and teach me how
> To name the bigger night, and how the less,
> That burn by day and night: and then I lov'd thee
> And show'd thee all the qualities o' th' isle,
> The fresh springs, brine-pits, barren place, and fertile.
> Cursed be I that did so!—All the charms
> Of Sycorax, toads, beetles, bats, light on you
> For I am all the subjects that you have,

1

> Which first was mine own king; and here you sty me
> In this hard rock, whiles you do keep from me
> The rest o' th' island.

There has been no agitator in all of colonial Africa to better Caliban's story and struggle. But theirs is a common theme so well developed in the literature of negritude and African personality that it need not delay us here.

The problem that Caliban shares with the African in English literature is not so much what both lost to the imperial lord as what they have gained from him, namely, the legacy of language:

> I pitied thee,
> Took pains to make thee speak, taught thee each hour
> One thing or the other: When thou didst not, savage,
> Know thine own meaning, but wouldst gabble like
> A thing most brutish, I endow'd thy purposes
> With words that made them known: but thy vile race,
> Though thou didst learn, had that in 't which good natures
> Could not abide to be with; therefore wast thou
> Deservedly confin'd into this rock
> Who hads't deserved more than a prison.

There is Prospero's own side of the story; he has taught the barbarian a civilized tongue in place of his native babble, has endowed him with a stock of words that makes his savage purposes known—known, that is, to Prospero and Miranda; for it is not as though Caliban possessed no language of his own before their arrival: he spoke one with Sycorax his mother. Still, Prospero has a case, and Mr Ian Smith and all race supremacists on both sides of the Atlantic cannot supply a more persuasive apology for their policies. But Caliban steers us back to course:

> You taught me language; and my profit on't
> Is, I know how to curse: the red plague gird you,
> For learning me your language!

Actually, Caliban is being gratuitously unfair to himself; he does not curse always, although his sense of disinheritance is obsessional and ubiquitous.

Caliban's 'imagination', says Wolfgang H. Clemen in *The Development of Shakespeare's Imagery*, 'is ruled by primitive needs of life, and this is expressed in his language'[1]. One might add that he is as much drunk with his second language, newly acquired at the hands of Prospero, as he is with the heady wine Stephano serves him at their meeting. Listen to him recommending his services to a new master he is scheming to stage-manage for his own ends:

> I'll show thee the best springs: I'll pluck thee berries;
> I'll fish for thee, and get thee wood enough.

Or listen to the following:

> I prithee, let me bring thee where crabs grow;
> And I with my long nails will dig thee pig nuts;
> Show thee a jay's nest and instruct thee how
> To snare the nimble marmozet, I'll bring thee
> To clust'ring filberts, and sometimes I'll get thee
> Young scamels from the rock.

When plotting the death of his old oppressor Prospero, it is the same torrent of words, the same lyric gush:

> Why, as I told thee, 'tis a custom with him
> I' the afternoon to sleep: there thou mayst brain him,
> Having first seized his books; or with a log
> Batter his skull, or paunch him with a stake,
> Or cut his wezand with the knife.

And when later his co-liberators and mercenaries are scared by the music of the invisible Ariel, listen to the words with which the savage soothes them:

> Be not afraid: the isle is full of noises,
> Sounds and sweet airs, that give delight, and hurt not;
> Sometimes a thousand twanging instruments
> Will hum about mine ears; and sometimes voices
> That, if I then had wak'd after long sleep,
> Will make me sleep again: and then, in dreaming,
> The clouds methoughts would open and show riches
> Ready to drop upon me; that when I wak'd
> I cried to dream again.

---

[1] *The Development of Shakespeare's Imagery* (London, Methuen, 1951).

It is little wonder then that Stephano, earlier on, for all his drunkenness, is struck instantly with surprise:

> This is some monster of the isle with four legs,
> Who hath got, as I take it, an ague.
> *Where the devil should he learn our language?*

The italics are mine. By 'our language' here the drunken butler means of course Italian, for after all, *The Tempest* is no straight English adventure story but one rendered or 'translated' by Shakespeare into English for his countrymen. But we are sailing ahead of the wind.

Stephano's surprise that Caliban, savage or monster, could speak fluent Italian is quite understandable. What perhaps is not so easily understandable is that several centuries after, many English readers, in their sober senses, are still not a little taken aback at the ability of the African to use the English language as a native speaker, even to the extent of writing poems, plays, and novels in it. Dylan Thomas, announcing the phenomenon of Amos Tutuola's *The Palm Wine Drinkard* to the British in 1952 wrote: 'a brief, thronged, grisly and bewitching story . . . written in English by a West African'. The emphasis, one could suspect, falls on the final statement, 'written in English by a West African' who being a native should write in his own vernacular. It is the first public admission of this linguistic prejudice by a prominent literary figure in Britain.

The implication seems to be that the new African literary performance is unusual, that it is unnatural for the African to write in English, French or Arabic. A decade after, does the point still arise? A debate is running right now but let us not get drawn into it. That the African has taken over a number of European languages is a fact of history, probably the one permanent evidence of the love–hate relationship today at play between Europe and Africa. English, French, Portuguese, and to a lesser extent, Spanish, and for an earlier period, Italian and German have become for Africans the language of government, business, education and indeed general communication, not simply between them and the wider world but in many cases among themselves at home as well as abroad. The situation is rather reminiscent of the earlier one in Europe when, before the formation of modern national states, her various peoples, with all their multiplicity of tongues, had for their common medium of expression Latin and Greek. But whereas the tendency then in Europe was towards homogeneous units, each adopting a vernacular as the language, the forces at work now in Africa have been for widely different groups to come together under one colonial flag and cosmopolitan language. Remove this dual experience of foreign rule and language and many of the new African states might well collapse without any help from military coups. Today each of these alien European tongues provides for many Africans the one ready vehicle for thought and even for dreaming. Recently there have been attempts to reverse the position, to replace the foreign with the vernacular tongue, notably in Tanzania where English has officially given way to Swahili. Elsewhere the African seems satisfied with having taken over a European tongue as he has the motor car, the radio, the refrigerator and all other articles of modern day living. After purchase, a ware becomes the *bona fide* property of the consumer.

There are a number of questions still to be answered. Having adopted a European language, how does the African writer use it, that is, with what sense of propriety? Does he fit the 'foreign' tongue to local subjects and characters? Is the language in his hands following the peculiar lie of the African situations that he depicts? As Hamlet would have put it, does the African writer in English or French 'suit the action to the word, the word to the action'? Or is there, as Mr A. Bodurin in *African Statesman* has charged, a dissociation of content from expression?[1]

This raises at once the old matter of verisimilitude. In the English or European novel and play there is observed a strict

---

[1] *African Statesman*, i, No. 1, Oct.–Dec. 1965.

gradation of speech according to social class, which in turn determines to a large extent the level of education and thought of each character. Notwithstanding the liberalization of opportunities and the greater degree of mobility now prevalent among the classes as a result of the adoption by Europeans of one brand of socialism or another, the peasant in Europe still remains a peasant, the office worker an office worker, and the factory hand a factory hand in the general scheme of things, each retaining an attitude of mind almost as unshakeable as the sense of security felt by the Elizabethan in the world picture of his time. The European artist, working within a norm like this, generally strives to achieve a naturalistic if individual reflection of life as lived in a chosen society.

Apparently for this reason, the African or native character in English literature has posed for the English writer a peculiar problem. How does he fit into the structure of a society where class and education determine a man's manner of speech and by implication the level of his mind as well as the limits which his ambition may vault?

Shakespeare provides the supreme example. In delineating Caliban, 'a savage and deformed slave', the dramatist does not rely on the simple use of dialect but on the quality and content of imagery. 'Caliban', to fall back on Wolfgang Clemen, 'is a person who does not think in abstract terms but in concrete objects, which consequently abound in his language.' And this is language learnt in adulthood and at the hand of a king whose own 'language has the widest range' from 'the familiar, conversational, easy-flowing tones' to 'the solemn poetic diction which has in it something dignified and lofty'. Caliban, we must remember, is no simple yokel straight out of the English countryside. Scandalized as Prospero is by Caliban's advances to Miranda, a sense of shock and outrage shared by nearly if not all European readers, it must not be forgotten that Caliban, though deformed and savage, was actually his own king before Prospero arrived and subverted him:

> For I am all the subjects that you have,
> Which first was mine own king.

The match therefore would have been an equal one uniting two royal houses in love and amity. But then there was the disparity of power, and of course Prospero's own political plans for his daughter and himself.

Othello and Aaron are Shakespeare's other natives. One wins general respect and sympathy: the other little or no notice except perhaps a little of that reluctant grudging admiration Iago arouses in us. Both however are Moors or black men, one and the same thing in Shakespeare as scholars like Dover Wilson have long maintained and Eldred Jones of Sierra Leone has lately demonstrated in his *Othello's Countrymen*. Unlike Caliban, they are not so much dispossessed in their own home as displaced persons, transplanted to a strange terrain in the manner of the American Negro, albeit with one qualification, an important one. Othello and Aaron are given opportunities by Venice and Rome to distinguish themselves in public life, a fact epitomized in the one winning the hand of Desdemona and the other the heart of Tamora. In contrast, the African, and the native Indian for that matter, remains in America a Caliban—a Caliban more in company of Stephano and Trinculo than of Prospero and of Miranda with whom he may not mate.

Of the close connection existing between Othello's speech and mind both Wolfgang Clemen and G. Wilson Knight have presented all the evidence there is. Aaron appears in a play in which Shakespeare has still to evolve this organic union between character and imagery; his is a language showing all the decorativeness of accumulative speech typical of the whole play. It can in fact be said with fairness that he seeks to impress all the time; that like Tamburlaine, if to a lesser degree, he sweeps his victims off their feet more by the force of his rhetoric than by his possession of any secret power. Probably the only characteristic betraying Shakespeare's belief in a common basic nature informing Othello and Aaron is the colourful, exotic quality of their imagery:

7

> I fetch my life and being
> From men of royal siege,

says Othello, when told of the impending attack on him by Branbantio whose daughter he has secretly married. Compare this to Aaron's one line asking Lucius for reprieve of his son when he has but short shrift himself:

> Touch not the boy; he is of royal blood.

Or hear Othello at the culmination of the so-called corruption scene, where the tide of damnation sweeps over the man and does not turn again until the very last, when he washes himself clean through remorse and self-sacrifice:

> Never, Iago: like to the Pontic sea,
> Whose icy current and compulsive course
> Ne'er feels retiring ebb, but keeps due on
> To the Propontic and the Hellespont;
> Even so my blood thoughts, with violent pace,
> Shall ne'er look back, ne'er ebb to humble love,
> Till that a capable and wide revenge
> Swallow them up. Now, by yond marble heaven,
> In the due reverence of a sacred vow
> I here engage my words.

And now listen to Aaron, also at the final turn of the tide in his phenomenal fortunes, in defence of his son:

> Now, by the burning tapers of the sky,
> That shone so brightly when this boy was got,
> He dies upon my scimitar's sharp point
> That touches this my first-born son and heir!
> I tell you, younglings, not Enceladus,
> With all his threatening band of Typhon's brood,
> Nor great Alcides, nor the god of war,
> Shall seize this prey out of his father's hands.

True, one is a noble character and the other an unrepentant villain, but both at the bottom are human beings touched by events where it hurts most, two men rallying to the defence of what they hold dearest in life—Othello his sense of honour, Aaron the safety of his son. Tone and movement in both passages, especially of colour and music, may be miles apart, which is no great surprise, considering the vast difference there is between the characters and roles of both men, and considering also the vast distance Shakespeare had still to cover between *Titus Andronicus* and *Othello*. Yet the belief in the magic of words, the more polyphonic the stronger, is very much present in the adopted language of these two black men playing for high stakes in a white land. Both are political figures assailing the very citadel of the state that holds them captive by a simple power of speech, which in eloquence anticipates the rhetoric of independence agitation in Africa, especially the brand inspired from the United States. It would be interesting too to compare the texture of Aaron's language with that of his professional and by far more proficient double, Iago. But more relevant here is a comparison of the following lines:

> I'll make you feed on berries and on roots,
> And feed on curds and whey, and suck the goat;
> And cabin in a cave, and bring you up
> To be a warrior, and command a camp

with these:

> I prithee, let me bring thee where crabs grow;
> And I with my long nails will dig thee pig nuts;
> Show thee a jay's nest and instruct thee how
> To snare the nimble marmozet, I'll bring thee
> To clustering filberts and sometimes I'll get thee
> Young scamels from the rock.

The first lines are Aaron's and the later ones of course come from our friend Caliban. The similarity in style and content is obvious. Barring the lingering ambition to return eventually to court, for Aaron, as delineated by Shakespeare who never really forgets the African's antecedents, it is the return to his natural state of primitive appetite and haunts, far from the sophisticated habits of his host. To recall Prospero's indictment of Caliban and all his brothers:

> But thy vile race,
> Though thou didst learn, had that in't which good natures
> Could not abide to be with.

9

After Shakespeare, the treatment by English writers of the speech habits of the savage or black man becomes less original and imaginative, approaching the stereotype successfully exploited by Negro spirituals. Mr. H. N. Fairchild in *The Noble Savage*, 'a study in romantic naturalism', gives a fair glimpse of the performance.[1] He begins with a description of the dialect used by two coloured characters in George Colman's *Inkle and Yarico*, a play produced and published in 1787:

> Both Yarico and Wowski have learned English . . . from a castaway who was subsequently eaten. Yarico speaks correctly except for the occasional omission of definite article(s). Wowski's English is decidedly broken; her misunderstanding of long words suggests that Colman thinks of her as a negress. Thus at the end of the play, when Trudge is taken into Governor Curry's service, we find:
>
> *Trudge:*   Wows, you'll be Lady, you jade to a Governor's Factotum.
>
> *Wowski:* Yes—I lady Jacktotum.
>
> That is hardly the speech of an Indian. But George Colman recked little of such refinements.

Mr Fairchild then gives the example of Leigh Hunt in his juvenile piece, 'The Negro Boy':

> Cold blows the wind, and while the tear
> Burst trembling from my swollen eye
> The rain's big drop quick meet it there,
> And on my naked bosom flies!
> O pity, all ye sons of Joy,
> The little wandering Negro Boy.

Except for the use here of 'tear burst' and 'quick meet', both probably poetic licences, the voice sounds educated if maudlin. A more interesting attempt at use of dialect described by Mr Fairchild was that by the humanitarian poet Amelia Opie in her propaganda piece 'The Negro Boy's Tale'.

---

[1] *The Noble Savage* (London, O.U.P., 1928).

10

Dey say me should to order do
Vat I would have dem do to me;
But, if dey preach and practise too;
A negro slave me should not be.

Missa, dey say dat our black skin
Be ugly, ugly to the sight;
But surely if dey look vidin,
Missa, de negro's heart be vite.

Ah missa! smiling in your tear
I see you know vat I'd impart;
De cocoa husk de skin I vear
De milk vidin be Zambo's heart.

Evidently, Zambo the Jamaican slave, moves his young mistress to tears, but as Mr Fairchild sums it up:

> One can hardly believe that Zambo's impossible speech added pathos or force to his criticism of society, for in that day the associations of dialect were broadly comical or satirical. I have found hardly any instances in which the Noble Savage of any hue speaks broken English. To make him do so would be to dispel the illusion that surrounds him. Man Friday though an Indian, talks like an eighteenth century literary negro. Colman's Wowski has a comical jargon for which again burlesques of negro speech are evident models. These cases, and a trace of dialect in the omitted article of 'And so I say to little English boy' in Blake's *Little Black Boy*, constitute the only exceptions that I have observed.

The Noble Savage, then, spoke mostly in standard English, as in William Cowper's 'The Negro's Complaint':

Why did all-creating Nature
    Make the plant for which we toil?
Sighs must fan it, tears must water,
    Sweat of ours must dress the soil.
Think, ye master iron-hearted,
    Looking at your jovial boards,
Think how many backs have smarted,
    For the sweets your cane affords.[1]

Cowper makes no attempt here at mimesis. He has for his subject the growing business of emancipation, and from

[1] 'The Negro's Complaint', *The Poetical Works of William Cowper* (London, O.U.P., 1967).

11

behind the mask of suffering we see on display, the voice is that of the poet himself, delivering a sermon in a straight period piece, just as Johnson does in *Rasselas*, probably the first work of fiction with an African hero and cast by a major author in English.

In prose, for several centuries until Joseph Conrad and Joyce Cary, and perhaps Graham Greene, the classic example of this so-called naturalistic school was to be found in Daniel Defoe's *Robinson Crusoe*:

> I had a mind once to try if he had any hankering inclination to his own country again; and having taught him English so well that he could answer me almost any question, I asked him . . . and so we began the following discourse:
>
> *Master*: You always fight the better? How came you to be taken prisoner then, Friday?
> *Friday*: My nation beat much for all that.
> *Master*: How beat? If your nation beat them, how came you to be taken?
> *Friday*: They more than my nation in the place where me was; they take one, two, three, and me; my nation overbeat them in the yonder place, where me no was, there my nation take one, two great thousand.
> *Master*: But why did not your side recover you from the hands of your enemies then?
> *Friday*: They run one, two, three and me, and make go in the canoe; my nation have no canoe that time.
> *Master*: Well, Friday, and what does your nation do with the men they take? Do they carry them away and eat them, as these did?
> *Friday*: Yes, my nation eats mans too; eat all up.

Present here are all the elements of the new dialect—broken syntax, incorrect inflection, derangement of word-order, reliance on repetition and on gesture as Defoe tells us later, when Friday, unable to count twenty in English, numbers the men he has eaten 'by laying so many stones in a row and pointing to me to tell them over'—all these with the possible exception of sound changes. Says Mr Fairchild: 'Friday's speech, which resembles that used in representations of Negro dialect in early American literature, makes it a little hard to remember that he is Carib.'

Here, our old problem arises again. How objective and realistic were these representations? An African learning English on a slave plantation, and a Carib learning it at the hands of a master, who is a sailor cut off from all contacts with his kind, will meet with a number of common difficulties; but a few others will be peculiar to each by reason of differences in their native languages. This however did not seem to have mattered to the English writer: to him both characters were one and the same phenomenon, a 'native', kin of Caliban, however different their tribes, coping as best as he could with a civilized tongue.

With the Negro in America the problem goes beyond this individual exercise; it becomes the experience of a whole group, a whole race forced to play a given role in society, attaining for itself in the course of time the status of a true dialect which, as the dictionary defines it, is a 'form of speech peculiar to a district, class, or person', in other words, a 'subordinate variety of a language with distinguishable vocabulary, pronunciation, or idioms'. This is the kind of thing attempted in *Uncle Tom's Cabin*.

> Say?—why, she kinder larfed in her eyes—dem great handsome eyes o' hern; and, says she, 'well, Aunt Chloe, I think you are about in the right on't,' says she; and she went off in de parlour. She oughter cracked me over de head for being so sarcy; but dar's what't is—I can't do nothin' with ladies in de kitchen![1]

Joseph Conrad's nigger on *The Narcissus*, a West Indian, 'enunciates distinctly, with a soft precision'. This is how he announces himself:

> I belong to the ship. The Captain shipped me this morning. I couldn't get aboard sooner. I saw you all aft as I came up the ladder, and could see directly you were mustering the crew. Naturally, I called out my name. I thought you had it on your list, and would understand. You misapprehended.[2]

[1] H. B. Stowe, *Uncle Tom's Cabin*.
[2] *The Nigger of the 'Narcissus'* (London, Heinemann, 1926).

13

A common sailor and nigger will not 'enunciate' like this, but the device suits the inscrutable theme of Conrad, who writes mystery into everything. His nigger in fact proves to be no common person:

> He held his head up in the glare of the lamp—a head vigorously modelled into deep shadows and shining lights—a head powerful and misshapen with a tormented and flattened face—a face pathetic and brutal: the tragic, the mysterious, the repulsive mask of a nigger's soul.[1]

Conrad probably had in mind a Rodin sculpture, the kind that moved Schweitzer to service; but masks, by the way, can be white, yellow or brown, reflective of all manners of spirits, and these need not be black to be tragic, mysterious, repulsive and possessed of any grade of soul.

In *Heart of Darkness* Conrad sheds no better light upon the matter. There the manager's African boy puts his insolent head in to make his famous announcement: 'Mistah Kurtz—he dead.' Conrad then, whose experience of English anticipates and parallels that of the African writer, fails to face up to the language problem as it affects 'natives' in English literature.

In contrast, Joyce Cary who was British and a colonial official in Nigeria, tried to tackle the problem. What success he achieved can be seen in *Mister Johnson*, believed by many to be his best African novel. Johnson, the absurd Nigerian clerk, wants a favour of the British official Mr Rudbeck:

> 'Yes, sah, please, A small small advance,'
> 'But I can't give advances, Mr Johnson. You know what would happen if I did. You'd be short next pay-day and simply get into debt.'
> 'Oh, sah, I think you give me.'[2]

Refused a pay advance, Johnson is in despair because he cannot meet his debts and marital commitments:

[1] Ibid.
[2] *Mister Johnson* (London, Michael Joseph, 1947).

> 'Oh, you bloody fool, Johnson—you no good for nutting—you see
> how bad stupid fool you are. Here's Mister Rudbeck you friend—de
> bes'man in de worl'—you only go to do your job proper, and dere
> you go making trouble for him all de time, I glad you get no rise—
> now 'haps you catch some sense—go throw yourself to the crocodiles.'[1]

In both extracts, decorum, as in the traditional novel, is
strictly observed—the language of the half-literate clerk who
learnt English as a second language clearly set off against the
superior accent of his boss and native speaker. In the soliloquy
Johnson maintains his proper level of expression. But only for
a while, for soon after, we hear him again, still addressing
himself in despair:

> 'I'm a fool. I'll take a knife and split myself up—that's all I'm worth.
> I'm a bad fool—I'll pour kerosene on my English suit and set myself
> on fire—I'm tired of myself.'[2]

Still in the same voice he goes on:

> 'And how am I going to pay for Bamu, and how am I going to pay
> the store. Why,' he says in a tone of astonishment, 'I'm done for—
> I'm finished—I'd better hang myself.'[3]

The transition is most astonishing, for it could well be Mr
Rudbeck himself speaking. Later, in the exchange between
Johnson and his 'bush' father-in-law, there is the same up-
grading of language:

> 'What do you want, father?'
> 'Nothing.'
> 'You want the ten shillings, I promised you?' The old man slowly
> raises his left hand and scratches his right armpit; at the same time
> he raises his chin and looks side-ways at the bush.
> 'Well, I haven't got it—I haven't got any money at all till the end
> of the month.'[4]

But immediately Johnson comes among his fellow workers
from southern Nigeria, he gravitates back to the hypocorism
assigned his race in the great tradition of English
literature:

[1] Ibid. [2] Ibid. [3] Ibid. [4] Ibid.

'Yes, I steal 'em.'
'You steal de keys?' Benjamin gazes at Johnson with dreaming wonder. 'How you do so?'
'Why, yass, Mister Benjamin—I think I go tonight—moon come up pretty late.'
'But Mister Rudbeck puts his keys under his pillow.'
'Yes, and his pistol,' Ajali cries. 'His revolver all loaded with bullets in every hole.'
'You tink I 'fraid, Ajali.'
'I think you better be 'fraid.'
'Perhaps you go to prison for a long time—many years.' Benjamin says.
'I tell you I get dem key tonight. Stay here—I show you.'[1]

Consistency—this is one of the rules not obeyed by Cary in his efforts at re-creating a natural dialogue for his African characters, and this fault might well be what puts off several of his African readers. There is no distinction among the four Johnsons we find speaking in the book—Johnson in conversation in English with the district commissioner and other English officials; Johnson in conversation with his compeers in the local lingua franca which is pidgin; Johnson in conversation with others in his vernacular, if he has any besides broken English; and Johnson in conversation with himself, that is, in monologue in the language most immediate to a specific subject or situation he happens to be in, this presumably being standard English, pidgin, or his vernacular.

The African writing in English has then before him on the one side the Shakespearean achievement, a poetic solution, and on the other the example of the naturalistic school that really is not so objective after all. He can either follow in the oversize footsteps of Shakespeare or adopt the devices of the naturalists. Better still, he can evolve his own approaches to the problem of language in his works. But first of all he must find for himself the right level of language before he chooses for his characters who in fact are his compatriots, brought up in the same environment, and fed upon the same diet of life. In other words, he stands in a relationship to his characters and subjects

[1] Ibid.

completely different from that obtaining for the English writer some of whose characters and situations happen to be African or 'native'. The African writer's view of his characters springs directly from the inside, unless he deliberately chooses to adopt a standpoint of seeing things from the outside. This might place him at a vantage point *to see the object as it really is*, or it may affect his vision in such a way that he fails *to see the object steadily and as a whole*. For the African writer then, the task of achieving verisimilitude is a little more complex than it seems for the English and for that matter, American and European writer.

Beginning as a matter of attitudes, the problem ties up intricately with that of form and communication. The artist, we said, must first find his own voice, and he has a choice of three as T. S. Eliot tells us of the poet in *The Three Voices of Poetry*:

> The first voice is the voice of the poet talking to himself—or to nobody. The second is the voice of the poet addressing an audience, whether large or small. The third is the voice of the poet when he attempts to create a dramatic character speaking in verse; when he is saying, not what he would say in his own person, but only what he can say within the limits of one imaginary character addressing another imaginary character.[1]

I am not at all sure that there is provision here for Cowper and his slave. A choice of one voice, James Joyce had stated much earlier in *Portrait of the Artist as a Young Man*, has the effect of determining the nature and form of the image the artist is seeking to forge:

> The image, it is clear, must be set between the mind or senses of the artist himself and the mind or senses of others. If you bear this in memory you will see that art necessarily divides itself into three forms . . . These are: the lyrical form, the form wherein the artist presents his image in immediate relation to himself; the epical form, the form wherein he presents his image in immediate relation to himself and to others; the dramatic form, the form wherein he presents his image in immediate relation to others.[2]

[1] *The Three Voices of Poetry* (London, C.U.P., 1953).
[2] *Portrait of the Artist as a Young Man* (London, Cape, 1950).

A number of factors govern this process of choice and formation which every artist undergoes consciously or subconsciously. First, the preparedness of the artist himself to assimilate and remould experience. Secondly, the fidelity of the artist towards the demands of each experience. And thirdly, the consideration for the public by the artist.

Preparedness involves more than talent. Everybody presumes the athlete possesses a certain natural ability which enables him to run faster, jump higher and farther as well as hurl objects to a greater distance than the ordinary man who pays to watch him perform. This is why if he has any sense of pride he enters the race at all. But to be really prepared, he must have undergone a certain degree of training. This in turn presupposes the availability of the right equipment and facilities. Of course there are and always will be natural winners. But barring accidents, the athlete has to be well equipped to perform well. So too with the artist. More basic still, if he is a carver, he must not only have the full use of his hands and eyes but also the knowledge to tell one piece of wood from another; and if he is a poet or musician, he must retain the full use of his tongue at all times—just as the athlete needs proper co-ordination of all his muscles.

With the plastic and oral arts the artist perfects his work by apprenticeship under a recognized master, by unceasing imitation of the master until he becomes his own model sought after by a fresh wave of novitiates. If there is abundance and continuation of talent over a considerable area and period, a great tradition, like that of the bronzes at Benin and the Ijala poetry of the Yoruba, will emerge. In contrast, the tradition of written literature as we know it, though partaking of elements drawing on the more ancient mediums of wood and voice, requires of the artist literacy and privacy. By literacy we mean that he must possess the right amount of schooling sufficient to make his readers forget the issue of education, while by privacy we mean the artist in the literate tradition not only works alone but makes use of masks wherever he can lay hands on them at the peril of being found out.

In the new literature of Africa written in a number of European languages the issue of literacy lies at the bottom of much of the criticism. We often hear it said that Africans writing in French are much more at home than Africans writing in English. Similarly, sophistication is supposed to be the special attribute of some African writers. All this seems to me mere backhanded compliment, indeed the old device of divide and rule. The implication is that one set of writers has still to overcome language difficulties, while the sophisticated chap but for this special grace would of course be a rustic, crude as the rest of his tribe. This raises a number of questions. Has there been over-education of Caliban? Is the cause of the difference that of under-education in the new language and medium? Or has Caliban acquired just the right dose of language and technique to cope with his trade, to practise the art of Prospero?

Fidelity towards the demands of a particular experience being ordered anew by the artist means that he must recognize immediately, indeed instinctively, the true nature and substance of the material and subject at his disposal. As the erector or assembler of an outfit that should act on the reader as a catalyst, is he himself serving as the medium to the experiment, or should he merely describe the process, or wholly leave the exercise to independent demonstrators to carry out? The first course entails the projection of the subject upon the screen of himself and consequently the production of a lyric piece. The second makes of him something of a commentatory man supplying a narrative. And the third leaves him completely out of the show, for then, having formulated what may be called a theoretical truth, the artist makes way for other experts to put it to the test, and the result is drama. Now only the pedant and purist will insist that all three courses are totally exclusive of one another. No work is so impersonal that it does not at some point carry upon it the pressure of the personality of its author and none is so personal that it does not possess an independent life of its own.

Fidelity to the dictates of experience goes beyond the form

that experience assumes in the act of being shaped for a purpose by the artist. There must also be fidelity to facts as they appear in such an experience, that is, the artist in the process of presentation should not fiddle with phenomena, for example, social manners, customs, costumes, and even more to our purpose, the quality of speech of a people.

In all this the artist operates in full or partial awareness of an audience. Said Wordsworth:

> ... by the act of writing ... an author makes a formal engagement that he will gratify certain known habits of association; that he not only thus apprises the reader that certain classes of ideas and expressions will be found in his book, but that others will be carefully excluded.[1]

As with all legal transactions, the contract calls for trust as well as thrust from both parties. The reader on the other side of it represents a public. This in extreme circumstances may be the artist himself or the immediate circle of his family and friends, but usually the public is the wider world outside. Now, a work of art, more so perhaps the literary piece, is like a pebble dropped into water. It creates its own ripples, with the shores of human experience for its limits. We may say the word is a pebble, better still a pearl, lying upon the bed of the stream of common speech. The artist picks it up to remould it, then drops it back into the common stream of human consciousness where it plumbs depths and stirs up ripples, awakening in our individual ponds of being waves of meaning and recognition.

It will be remembered that Wordsworth prided himself in being a man speaking to men in the actual day-to-day language used by them. But for all his missionary zeal of wanting to bring poetry to the people, his ballads did not reach beyond his own traditional, fixed class of men, enjoying a set of preferences. Today his successors, though at work in a much more diffuse society, write for a still more or less defined audience, an audience based primarily at home.

[1] 'Preface to Lyrical Ballads', *The Prelude*.

Not so the African writing in one of several European languages. Right from the start, he labours to please a dual audience, a sector of which is in Europe, where he has most of his books published, and the other sector at home among his own people whose chronicler he is in effect. His peculiar problem then is to give satisfaction to members of both sides, each with its own set of habits and tastes.

For a variety of reasons, the European section has been more articulate and of overwhelming influence upon African writers. Jealously, it holds fast to its claim of being the original owner, and therefore the natural custodian of the European language the African is using in his works. These in turn belong to the tradition of literate literature which again goes back to Europe. The very machinery for publication and distribution of African works is to be found chiefly in the capital cities of Europe. Then of course there is the old economic supremacy, ever more in ascendance as open political power appears to be on the decline, and the attendant fact that the European reader generally possesses a greater buying power than the African. Finally, there are the agents of this ubiquitous complex operating right in the midst of the African sector, and ironically the scouts and promoters of new talents are often to be found among their ranks. The net effect is the imposition of their standards upon African writing. Out of this comes a smug sense of expectation of what the African writer can and should achieve—but expectation is sister to prediction, and any art that can be pre-determined has no place for experiment or the progressive exploration of the human spirit.

One such imposed standard has central bearing upon our search—that of the uses of language in the new poetry, drama, and fiction of Africa. It affects most of all the genre of fiction. This probably has to do with a point we made some years ago in an odd essay in *Nigeria* that of all the literary genres the novel happens to be the only one that Africa has borrowed from Europe. The new playwright in Africa, though employing a European idiom and technique, plies a traditional art form. So too with the modern African poet, who incidentally is a lyric artist, singing and speaking of experiences and problems immediately personal to him. Consequently, he has not as yet produced any ballad or epic. For the narrative work, presenting a subject in medial relation to artist and audience, we have to go to the novelist. His is the one form of literature that belongs strictly to the European literate tradition; author and reader must both be literate to enter into Wordsworth's contract. Furthermore, far from being a performing, aural, and communal art as with story-telling, poetry, and drama in Africa, it is not a shared form but one limited to an individual visual experience, one that is private and silent between artist and reader. Finally, even in Europe, the example of *Ulysses* and the French *nouveaux romans* notwithstanding, the novel seems to be the only literary form of note to retain the old rules. Our search for the African writer's approach to his adopted European tongue will accordingly be limited to his performance in this truly 'foreign' form.

The old canon of propriety, we have seen, required all characters to speak according to the dialect of their class and education. In a society where these distinctions do not prevail, a canon like this really cannot hold, for then to observe in art what does not exist in life would be, unless one is creating fantasy, to break the other canon of verisimilitude which demands that there shall be no falsification of the facts, social or otherwise. The fact of language in Ijaw, as we have said on several occasions, is that stratification, where it exists, works first along the lines of geography and clan, a purely linguistic phenomenon, then along differences of proficiency prevalent everywhere among individual speakers of all languages on earth, for example, those that cut one man out of many in Ijaw for the role of *bebe-are-owei*, that is orator or spokesman for a town or clan. Stratification then within a clan in Ijaw, where all men speak one and the same language with a syntax, accent, lexis and register held in common and equal stock, is a matter of art and rhetoric. This seems to be the situation with a majority, if not all, of the languages and societies in Africa south of the Sahara.

The rôle of the author writing of a society like this in an adopted language therefore appears to me to be one quite similar to that of the letter-writer. If he is writing in vernacular, his task will be simply to take dictation as a good secretary, but if, as is often the case in Nigeria, the letter-writer himself is literate only in English, then it is his duty to render the message of his client in an equivalent English reflecting the true state and quality of his mind. If the scribe is worth his salt, he will record the actual flow, images and any devices of speech used by his client to convey the true content of the message. To employ pidgin English or some such patois because his client is an Urhobo farmer or an Ijaw fisherman writing to his son in the city or petitioning the government against a wrong, would be to do him the worst of wrongs.

This is why the Shakespearean solution seems to me the supreme example for the African writer in a European language to follow. It makes it possible to tell Caliban from Othello simply by comparing the imagery and themes predominant in their language. In the same way it should be possible to tell the Ibo farmer Okonkwo in Mr Achebe's *Things Fall Apart* from the Ijaw fisherman, Zifa in my *Song of a Goat*: references of the one naturally incline more to barnyards and harvests as those of the other to fishlines and tides. Pursued with sympathy and diligence, the method will not only reveal differences of character among them but delineate the contour and colour of one given setting as against another, say, the Sahara as distinct from the Niger Delta, one carrying a barren, perhaps, nomadic flavour, and the other the smell of swamps and the echo of the sea.

The study of the uses of language in a literary work lends itself to such discoveries because language in fact, as acknowledged by linguists, provides the best index to a people's culture, that totality of activity they learn and share together within the area of their settlement throughout their lifetime. With non-literate people, this can be very concrete. Says Edward Sapir in *Language*:

> The use of language in cultural accumulation and historical trans-
> mission is obvious and important. This applies not only to sophisti-
> cated levels but to primitive ones as well. A great deal of the cultural
> stock in trade of a primitive society is presented in a more or less
> well-defined linguistic form. Proverbs, medicine formulae, stan-
> dardized prayers, folk tales, standardized speeches, song texts,
> genealogies are some of the overt forms which language takes as a
> culture-preserving instrument.[1]

A study of themes will also yield similar interesting results.
Man everywhere lives the same basic thoughts, emotions, and
desires. All the same, what is *leit-motiv* for one kind of people
in one place at one time may not be for another group. For
example, gadgets, stocks, democracy and sex seem the main
moving forces in life for many an American; for the Nigerian,
at least until the soldiers stepped in, diplomas, politics, ritual
and reproduction. The British, having lost their driving spirit
since the interment of the Empire, are today busy searching
for it at home under the table, in the kitchen sink, in the water
closet, and over the beaches across the Channel into Europe.
Sucked into such a search, the British Sunday sibyl Penelope
Gilliat can be pardoned for being impatient with an Ijaw
fisherman who loses the will to live when he loses potency and
all hope of further procreation. His surely is a tragic passion
as the Greeks knew it, and as only primitive people today, like
Garcia Lorca's and mine, may know it.

A stress upon the study of language texture and leading
themes as a means for indexing character and situation in the
African novel, play and poem does not mean the complete
dismissal of the more popular method exploited by the
'naturalists'. Graded speech which defines the relative superiority of social stations among characters, and perhaps their
geophysical locations has in fact its own place in modern
African literature. Where appropriately used, pidgin or
broken English, for instance, serves to show up the new order
of things, with differences of education and employment
opportunites creating a variety of social classes among the

---

[1] *Language* (London, Hart-Davies, 1963).

polyglot populations ineluctably on the move today from the rural areas to the urban.

The novelist Mr Chinua Achebe combines both methods to great advantage. He uses in the main the Shakespearean approach, supplementing it with that of 'propriety' whenever necessary. But first it must be noted that Mr Achebe is eminently qualified for his task. Right from his first novel *Things Fall Apart* to his fourth uncanny work *A Man of the People*, he has found for himself a voice of balanced tones, adequate for his purposes, faithful to the facts, and fair to all sections of his readership. As a result, the text of each of his novels is an integrated piece, free of undue pressure from the personality of the artist who maintains all the time a medial distance between his subject and audience:

> Obierika was sitting outside under the shade of an orange tree making thatches from leaves of the raffia palm. He exchanged greetings with Okonkwo and led the way into his obi.[1]

This is a passage from *Things Fall Apart*. It shows how in a straight prose text, whether narrative, descriptive or expository, Mr Achebe can place things with surprising ease and brevity. This economy of expression and the impregnation of it with the spirit of the matter informing the subject is probably Mr Achebe's contribution to the novel, and it is nothing less than a consummate use of imagery.

The use of proverbs forms of course an aspect of this, but the tendency among critics has been to dwell on that alone. In so doing, the overall texture and tenor of Mr Achebe's language has not had the full attention it deserves. In 'English and the African Writer', Mr Achebe himself gives a superb illustration of what the language becomes in his hands:

> Allow me to quote a small example from *Arrow of God* which may give some idea of how I approach the use of English . . . The Chief Priest is telling one of his sons why it is necessary to send him to Church: 'I want one of my sons to join these people and be my eyes there. If there is nothing in it you will come back. But if there is

[1] *Things Fall Apart* (London, Heinemann, 1958).

something there you will bring home my share. The world is like a Mask, dancing. If you want to see it well you do not stand in one place. My spirit tells me that those who do not befriend the white man today will be saying had we known tomorrow.'

Now supposing I had put it another way, like this for instance: 'I am sending you as my representative among these people just to be on the safe side in case the new religion develops. One has to move with the times or else one is left behind. I have a hunch that those who fail to come to terms with the white man may well regret their lack of foresight.'[1]

Mr Achebe then concludes:

The material is the same. But the form of the one is in character and the other is not. It is largely a matter of instinct, but judgement comes into it too.[2]

The proverb remains in all this a powerful implement to till the interior being of a people with no literate means to stock memory, and Mr Achebe wields it very adroitly in and out of the line of dialogue:

Seven years was a long time to be away from one's clan. A man's place was not always there waiting for him. As soon as he left, someone else rose and filled it. The clan was like a lizard; if it lost its tail it soon grew another.[3]

Proverbs add speed and spice to speech and thought—even on the lips of Okonkwo who is not a great one with words:

'If I had a son like him I should be happy. I am worried about Nwoye. A bowl of pounded yam can throw him in a wrestling match. His two younger brothers are more promising. But I can tell you, Obierika, that my children do not resemble me. Where are the young suckers that will grow when the old banana tree dies? If Ezinma had been a boy I would have been happier. She has the right spirit.'

'You worry yourself for nothing,' said Obierika. 'The children are still very young.'

'Nwoye is old enough to impregnate a woman. At his age I was already fending for myself. No, my friend, he is not too young. A chick that will grow into a cock can be spotted the very day it

1 'English and the African Writer', *Transition*, iv, no. 18.
2 Ibid.
3 *Things Fall Apart*, op cit.

hatches. I have done my best to make Nwoye grow into a man, but there is too much of his mother in him.'[1]

A device taken for granted in adult speech, the proverb can show up the forward youth or the pompous person, for example, 'one of the older members' of the Umuofia Progressive Union Lagos in *No Longer at Ease*:

'Everything you have said is true. But there is one thing I want you to learn. Whatever happens in this world has a meaning. As our people say: "Whatever something stands, another thing stands by it." You see this thing called blood. There is nothing like it. That is why when you plant yam it produces another yam, and if you plant an orange it bears oranges. I have never yet seen a banana tree yield a cocoyam. Why do I say this? You young men here, I want you to listen because it is from listening to old men that you learn wisdom. I know that when I return to Umuofia I cannot claim to be an old man. But here in this Lagos I am an old man to the rest of you.' He paused for effect. 'This boy that we are all talking about, what has he done? He was told that his mother died and he did not care. It is a strange and surprising thing, but I can tell you that I have seen it before. His father did it.' There was some excitement at this.
'Very true', said another old man.
'I say that his father did the same thing', said the first man very quickly, lest the story be taken from his mouth. 'I am not guessing and I am not asking you to question it outside. When his boy's father—you know him, Isaac Okonkwo—when Isaac Okonkwo heard of the death of his father he said that those who kill with matchet must die by the matchet.'
'Very true', said the other man again.[2]

A similar device of imagery is that of the tale or parable suddenly thrown in to light up the core of a discussion:

"Tortoise went on a long journey to a distant clan. But before he went he told his people not to send for him unless something new under the sun happened. When he was gone, his mother died. The question was how to make him return to bury his mother. If they told him that his mother had died, he would say it was nothing new. So they told him that his father's palm tree had borne a fruit at the end of its leaf. When tortoise heard this, he said he must return

[1] Ibid.
[2] *No Longer at Ease* (London, Heinemann, 1960).

27

home to see this great monstrosity. And so his bid to escape the
burden of his mother's funeral was foiled."

There was embarrassed silence when Nathaniel finished his story.[1]

The embarrassed silence was not just because the story that
had been meant for a few ears had become the listening point
for all, but because it shed an epiphanic light upon the plight
of Obi Okonkwo. Together with the proverb, the tale is one
of the peculiar devices Mr Achebe adopts as the principle for
his art—almost in the same spirit as Hopkins elected to use
sprung rhythm for his poetry, a familiar device but one never
so consistently used before. In *Arrow of God* the principle is
so rigorously applied that there are those who would say
enough should have been enough.

The new social attitudes and distinctions obtaining in mixed
urban life are well reflected by Mr Achebe's use of pidgin
English and other modes of language. Before the Lagos Branch
of the Umuofia Progressive Union meeting on December 1
1956, Joseph rings up Obi on the telephone:

> 'You will not forget to call for me?' he asked.
>
> 'Of course not', said Obi. 'Expect me at four.'
>
> 'Good! see you later.' Joseph always put on an impressive manner
> when speaking on the telephone. He never spoke Ibo or pidgin
> English at such moments. When he hung up he told his colleagues:
> 'That na my brother. Just return from overseas. B.A. (Honours)
> Classics.' He always preferred the fiction of Classics to the truth of
> English. It sounded more impressive.
>
> 'What department he de work?'
>
> 'Secretary to the Scholarship Board.'
>
> 'E go make plenty money there. Every student who wan' go England
> go see am for house.'
>
> 'E no be like dat', said Joseph. 'Him na gentleman. No fit take bribe'.
>
> 'Na so', said the other in disbelief.[2]

Pidgin gives bite to the class war still gathering force in the
urban areas as when an under-privileged patient dresses Obi
down for jumping the queue at a clinic:

[1] Ibid.
[2] Ibid.

> 'You tink because Government give you car you fit do what you like? You see all of we de wait here and you just go in. You tink na play we come play?'
> Obi passed on without saying a word.
> 'Foolish man. He tink say because him get car so derefore he can do as he like. Beast of no nation!'[1]

Pidgin is not the speciality of the low income group. Not only can the master mix it with the domestic, but so-called educated persons of the same class and ethnic group will resort to it in intimate conversation as happens frequently in *A Man of the People*:

> 'Wetin you fit cook?' asked Chief Nanga as he perused the young man's sheaf of testimonials, probably not one of them genuine.
> 'I fit cook every European chop like steak and kidney pie, chicken puri, misk grill, cake omlette . . .'
> 'You no sabi cook African chop?'
> 'Aha! That one I no sabi am—o', he admitted. 'A no go tell master lie.'
> 'Wetin you de chop for your own house?' I asked, being irritated by the idiot.
> 'Wetin I de chop for my house?' he repeated after me. 'Na we country chop I de chop.'
> 'You country chop no be African chop?' asked Chief Nanga.
> 'Na him', admitted the cook. 'But no be me de cook am. I get wife for house.'
> My irritation vanished at once and I joined Chief Nanga's laughter. Greatly encouraged the cook added: 'How man wey get family go begin enter kitchen for make bitterleaf and egusi? Unless if the man no get shame.'[2]

It will be remembered that Chief Nanga is a Minister of State after long serving his nation as a teacher, and that the narrator John Odili is a university graduate who takes himself quite seriously. All the same, when he goes to arrange to pick up a young female nurse at some hospital, both boy and girl drop the stiff accent of standard English to assume the familiar nuance and tang of pidgin:

[1] Ibid.
[2] *A Man of the People* (London, Heinemann, 1966).

29

> 'Na lie', she said, smiling her seductive, two-dimpled smile. 'The
> way I look you eye I fit say that even ten Elsies no fit belleful you'.
> 'Nonesense', I said. 'Abi den take Elsie make juju for me?' I asked,
> laughing.
> 'I know?' she shrugged.
> 'You suppose to know', I said.[1]

One reservation may be made here—this is pidgin English as
spoken in Eastern Nigeria, a blend between standard English
and pure pidgin 'as it is spoke' in its other home outside
Freetown and Western Cameroun, which is Warri.

Of greater interest is the particular brand of English spoken
by Chief Nanga, Minister of Culture:

> 'Look here, Odili', he turned on me then like an incensed leopard,
> 'I will not stomach any nonsense from any small boy for the sake
> of a common woman, you hear? If you insult me again I will show
> you pepper. You young people of today are very ungrateful. Imagine!
> Anyway don't insult me again—o . . .'[2]

The idiom here carries the ethos of a whole epoch, a language
that some linguists have labelled Nigerian English.

A resource of language left Mr Achebe to exploit fully is
the double-talk perfected by the early interpreter between the
white man and the African community. Often a 'native' himself, the interpreter was a functionary enjoying special influence in the old colonial system. What decision the white
district officer, a veritable Pooh-bah, arrived at in a case in
court depended largely upon how it was presented to him by
the interpreter, although his usually was para-English. And
the farther he stood from the white man in the act of delivery,
the higher soared his reputation among the local people—for
a man so much at home with the 'haw-haw' of the white man
at such great distance must possess strange powers of understanding indeed! Mr Achebe touches on the subject in *Things
Fall Apart*:

> 'What has happened to that piece of land in dispute?' asked
> Okonkwo.

[1] Ibid.
[2] Ibid.

'The white man's court has decided that it should belong to Nnama's family, who had given much money to white man's messengers and interpreter.'
'Does the white man understand our custom about land?'
'How can he when he does not even speak our tongue?'[1]

The lack of a direct common language between the strangers and natives of Umuofia contributed in no small way to things falling apart in the clan. It created dramatic situations still waiting to be tapped by the novelist and playwright. The possibilities are clearly there as can be seen in Mr Achebe's third novel *Arrow of God*. The scene is the new road the white man is building by direct compulsory labour of the young of the clan:

Unachukwu translated:
'Tell them this bloody work must be finished by June.'
'The white man says that unless you finish this work in time you will know the kind of man he is.'
'No more lateness.'
'Pardin?'
'Pardon what? Can't you understand plain, simple English? I said there will be no more late-coming.'
'Oho. He says everybody must work hard and stop all this shit-eating.'
'I have one question I want the white man to answer.' This was Nweke Ukpaka.
'What's that?'
Unachukwu hesitated and scratched his head.
'Dat man wan axe master queshon!'
'No questions.'
'Yessah.' He turned to Nweke. 'The white man says he did not leave his house this morning to come and answer your questions.'
The crowd grumbled. Wright shouted that if they did not immediately set to work they would be seriously dealt with. There was no need to translate this; it was quite clear.[2]

The other occasion is when the priest Ezeulu is led out of prison before the white district officer to be offered high public office, the same progress that many a colonial leader would

[1] *Things Fall Apart*, op. cit.
[2] *Arrow of God* (London, Heinemann, 1964).

make several years later at the dismemberment of the Empire:

> 'Your name is Ezeulu?' asked the interpreter after the white man had spoken.
> This repeated insult was nearly too much for Ezeulu but he managed to keep calm.
> 'Did you not hear me? The white man wants to know if your name is Ezeulu!'
> 'Tell the white man to go and ask his father and his mother their names.'
> There followed an exchange between the white man and his interpreter. The white man frowned his face and then smiled and explained something to the interpreter who then told Ezeulu that there was no insult in the question.
> 'It is the way the white man does his own things.'[1]

Scenes and exchanges like these make one a little more appreciative of the melodrama and opera that was the Indirect Rule of Lord Lugard.

If Mr Achebe is a highly accomplished notary enjoying wide practice in both city and countryside, then Mr Amos Tutuola is a village letter-writer without the benefit of a formal education, relying solely on his natural gifts. That he had not solved his own personal problem of voice and expression with his adopted tongue is acknowledged by his editor in his first and truly famous work *The Palm Wine Drinkard*. There, a page of the original manuscript is put on display in the state it arrived at the publishers:

> I could not blame the lady for following the skull as a complete gentleman to his house at all, because if I were a lady, no doubt, I would follow him to wherever he would go, and still as I was a man I would jealous him more than that, because if this gentleman go to the battle field, surely, enemy will not kill him or capture him and if bombers see him in a town which was to be bombed, they would not throw bombs on his presence, and if they throw it, the bomb itself would not explode until this gentleman would leave that town, because of his beauty . . .[2]

---

[1] Ibid.
[2] *The Palm Wine Drinkard* (London, Faber, 1952).

Now compare this with the 'corrected' version: the run-on form *atall* has been separated, *would go* and *see* have given way to *went* and *saw*, *throw* has the auxiliary *did* to fill it out, and there are the changes of punctuation. Why the editors felt it necessary to improve upon a part of the syntax while leaving the rest intact is still one of the mysteries of English publishing of African authors.

All through this operation Mr Tutuola remains faithful to his vision, a most compelling one. Even more winning is his complete lack of self-consciousness in this first novel. It completely bowled over the English critics. The fascination it held for Dylan Thomas can now be better understood against a background of the man's own belief in the bizarre magic and mesh of language as revealed in his poetry and recently published letters. But unlike Thomas or the much greater Joyce, Mr Tutuola did not consciously set out to probe further into the depths of man by re-organizing afresh the language he knew too well to be exhausted to accept again as an efficient tool to record, explore and extend experience. His in fact provides a concrete case of the 'natural' performing in the one style known to him. Later when he grows self-conscious and avails himself of the services of a postal tutorial course in English, we can see the results for what they really are as in his *Feather Woman of the Jungle*:

> Her body was downy but she wrapped herself from knees to the waist with the skin of a tiger and the rest parts were soft feathers. The feathers were really grown out from her body except her head which had white thick hair. Her eyes were red and hollow with old age. Her breasts were hardly to see because soft feathers were covered them. Almost all her teeth had fallen out so that made her mouth to be moving up and down always as if she was eating something in the mouth.[1]

This is most graphic; in fact it reminds one of Igor Stravinsky's *Fire Bird*, but although there is less work for his editors to do, the grammatical horns are sticking out still; nor has the dialogue lost anything of its stiffness and artificiality:

[1] *Feather Woman of the Jungle* (London, Faber, 1968).

33

> As we were still wondering and trembling with fear from feet to head, she started to ask with a fearful, huge and weak voice: 'What do both of you come to do in my land or do you not know that this is my jungle?' I answered at the same time with a trembling voice, 'We are sorry to come to your jungle, old woman. But I shall be glad if you will spare me if a few minutes more just to explain to you of what we were finding about before we came to your jungle.'[1]

Here is no original language as such but one to be found everywhere in Nigeria in the letters and 'compositions' written among a vast group of people who for various reasons have not proceeded beyond a certain stage of school. It is a level of English considered 'vulgar', half-illiterate by all sections of Nigerian society, and it is for this reason parents disapprove of their children reading Tutuola! What distinguishes Mr Tutuola's language is the ubiquity and omnigeneity of his imagery. Mr Janheiz Jahn in *Muntu*, declaring that 'Tutuola writes English without taking over the way of thinking characteristic of European languages', describes this very well:

> He fits European objects, modern customs, even economic forms seamlessly into his mythological world. Taxes are paid there—for the rental of fear; death is purchased for £70 18s 6d; a terrible voice sounds out of a big tank; then a 'half-bodied child' speaks lightly 'like a telephone'. In the hall of the merciful mother, a kind of fool's paradise, all the lights are in technicolour and change every five minutes. The sober materials of the technological age are transformed in these strange contexts and are turned from objects of technology into magic . . . and since Tutuola sees everything from the point of view of function, this distorts the original thing in ironical fashion.[2]

It may be said of Mr Tutuola that his depiction of a world largely mythological with technological imagery, like bombs, clocks, and radios, represents his hallmark as an artist just as the use of the proverb to advance ideas in what really are novels of ideas characterizes Mr Achebe. To this may be added what Mr Jahn, citing the 'complete gentleman' passage above 'as an example of prose rhythm', calls Tutuola's

[1] Ibid.
[2] *Muntu* (London, Faber, 1961).

sense of rhythm. Rhythm here, however, is not so much the segmentation in time of a whole but the 'repetition of a fact, of gesture, of words that form a *leit-motiv*—establishing in the story the extraordinary beauty of the scarecrow for whom the shrew falls at last. This 'rhythmical kind of narrative in which the repetition intensifies the dramatic quality of the action, makes Tutuola's story oral literature.' Accordingly, as Mr Léopold Sedar Senghor says of the African poem, the drinkard's story 'as it appears before our eyes in print is therefore incomplete, if it is not given rhythm at least through a percussion instrument'. But to conclude from here that 'Tutuola has created the purest expression so far of neo-African prose' is to pass judgement from that same bench which pronounced that 'only (negritude) poetry was legitimate' in Africa.

'Naïveté', made so much of by the adulators of Mr Tutuola and incidentally by the followers of the Onitsha market novelette, is not enough; language has to be 'moulded' by the artist with skill and consciousness. Mr Tutuola who lacks both of these qualities in his early work sacrifices something of his natural charm and power by trying to acquire them in his later works. It is as if the Onitsha market novelist were to aspire to the equipment of an Achebe! Mr Tutuola's difficulties with lexis and syntax remain unresolved. Now while Mrs Malaprop habitually mistakes one word for another resembling it, Mr Tutuola rarely does so, and then it is to create a completely new form out of an ill-understood one as in the title word *drinkard*, itself a new addition to the language. More typical of him is the use of one inflected form for another of the same root, for example, *hardly* and *were covered* in 'her breasts were hardly to see because soft feathers were covered them'. Such predilection and weakness do not make him 'purely African', and far from contributing to the man's magic fascination for us as a compulsive story-teller, actually detract from it. It is because he suffers open handicaps here that his is said to be no language for others to imitate, being essentially a *tour de force* or possibly a hoax.

In contrast, Mr Gabriel Okara attempts in *The Voice* a

35

language which his publishers proudly proclaim 'deliberately reproduces the rhythms of the African vernacular'.

> *Third Messenger*: Your nonsense words stop. These things have meaning no more so stop talking words that create nothing.
>
> *First Messenger*: Listen not to him. He speaks this word always because he passed standard six. Because he passed standard six his ears refuseth nothing, his inside refuseth nothing like a dustbin.
>
> *Third Messenger* (angrily): *Shut your mouth. You know nothing.*
>
> *First Messenger* (also angrily): Me know nothing? Me know nothing. Because I went not to school I have no bile, I have no head? Me know nothing? Then answer me this. Your hair was black black be, then it became white like a white cloth and now it is black black be more than blackness . . .[1]

Needless to say, the Ijaws all come off badly in the exercise, the author included. With commands and requests like 'Your nonsense words stop' Mr Okara is no doubt trying to recreate the original sentence structure of object–verb, but he has no justification for converting the normal subject–object–verb order of straight statements. Similarly, he has no cause to resort to the biblical verb ending -eth, very rare as plural even in Elizabethan usage, and the odd use of both the negative and verb to be. The result is not the reproduction of Ijaw rhythms in English but an artificial stilted tongue, more German than Ijaw. It is a creation completely devoid of the positive attractions of a living language like pidgin English.

That Mr Okara himself appears dissatisfied with his efforts can be seen in his own failure to apply the method consistently. Very often he lapses into regular English patterns as in the italicized portions of the passage quoted above. He in fact does so for a great stretch of the story, and what little success he achieves in the novel is to be found in such areas where he forgets himself as 'the artful forger' and becomes his true self, an artist discarding all gimmickry:

[1] *The Voice* (London, Deutsch, 1968).

> When day broke the following day it broke on a canoe aimlessly floating down the river. And in the canoe tied together back to back with their feet tied to the seats of the canoe were Okolo and Tuere. Down they floated from one bank of the river to the other like debris, carried by the current. Then the canoe was drawn into a whirlpool. It spun round and round and was slowly drawn into the core and finally disappeared. And the water rolled over the top and the river flowed smoothly over it as if nothing had happened.[1]

A passage like this gives immediate pleasure, opens for the reader a fresh window upon the world around us and consequently establishes its own validity as a product of art.

One significant lesson emerges from this kind of experiment. Images can be transplanted from one language into another. It is possible too to translate and transfer special words as well as idiomatic expressions. Mr Okara occasionally does this with renderings like the *it* of the story, which is the Ijaw, *iye*, meaning from the most to the least tangible of things. He does the same with the term *inside* which is *biri*, the belly as the seat of human passion and will. His use of the expression 'Your head is not correct' derives also directly from Ijaw idiom and usage. All this can be done and with profit as we saw in the case of Mr Achebe. But any attempt to superimpose the rhythm, syntax, and structure of one language upon another, especially where one is tonal and the other inflected, will remain at best a quixotic quest.

Mr Okara's experiment with *The Voice* offers then this conclusive proof: for the African writer in a European language, the use of external and formalistic devices like special syntax and sentence-structures from the vernacular, although tempting, carries with it risks that can lead even the genius to disaster. As a corollary, his best way to a new and genuine mode of expression seems to lie in a reliance upon the inner resources of language. These are images, figures of meaning and speech, which with expert handling can achieve for his art a kind of blood transfusion, reviving the English language by the living adaptable properties of some African language.

[1] Ibid.

The African writer thus occupies a position not unlike that of the ambidextrous man, a man placed in the unique and advantageous position of being able to draw strength from two separate equal sources. His is a gift of tongues. So equipped, he should be able to meet the exacting demands of both sectors of his audience. But if he fails, he will end up like Caliban crying:

> I shall be pinch'd to death————

and goodness knows the critic can be vicious, even like Prospero and his pack of spirits forever hounding Caliban, so that the African writer may well cry out with his ancestor:

> For every trifle are they set upon me.
> Sometime like apes, that mow and chatter at me
> And after bite me; they like hedge-hogs, which
> Lie tumbling in my bare-feet way and mount
> Their pricks at my foot-fall; sometime am I
> All wound with adders, who with cloven tongues
> Do kiss me into madness.

2: Themes of African poetry of English expression

In June 1964 I was in Moscow attending a Writers' Conference convened by the editors of *Foreign Literature* and *Problems of Literature*, two influential voices within the Union of Soviet Writers. The conference theme was 'Problems of literature in the developing nations of Africa and Asia' of which the Soviet Union is a proud member. Arriving a day late, and not armed with a brief from the Society of Nigerian Authors which I was representing, I thought to myself discretion would be the better part of valour and that the best active thing I could do in the two days of the conference would be to cultivate peaceful co-existence with as many delegates as came my way, the majority of them from the other side of the so-called Iron Curtain then being painfully redrawn to exclude China.

But what happened? Alone at this ostensible gathering of friends, I was soon singled out for attack by a solid bloc of Soviet womanhood, all draped in black—Professor Galperina they called her. 'Why are Nigerian poets, several of them the best in English-speaking Africa, so opposed to negritude, an ideology that has inspired their French-speaking counterparts like President Léopold Sedar Senghor of Senegal and his old comrade from the West Indies, Aimé Césaire? Was it right of your compatriot Wole Soyinka to laugh at negritude by asking whether or not the tiger proclaims its tigritude? Are you Nigerian poets happy with the Penguin people's grouping of you into a cult of personality? Is this not an escape—a denial of the society to which you ought to be giving full service with all your undoubted poetic talents?'

Questions on the West African folktale and the new fiction of Africa then followed free from two other women professors, again very well-informed and full of fire. Altogether their combined performance must have been regarded by all there as providing a fine barrage of indefensible missiles, for the hall that was all stupor and droning before became charged with life and alert to the grave state of danger facing my country and continent in the form of their own selfish poets. I could have run for cover in some fall-out shelter had there been one in sight. So feeling very much exposed, I decided to make a stand of it before the sustained force of those veritable furies. And so I should like to do now, for the wind though blowing from a different direction seems to me pretty much the same.

First, let us try and define our field so that we can at least remain on *terra firma*! English is the common language spoken in the five West African countries of Gambia, Sierra Leone, Liberia, Ghana and Nigeria as well as in the three East African states of Kenya, Uganda and Tanzania where Swahili has become an alternative official language. English also is the language of business and government in the three Central African nations of Malawi, Zambia and of the thorny territory of Rhodesia to their south. Still further down, English offers the one relatively hopeful face to the Janus-figure of South Africa fixated in its terrible Boer vision which refuses to change its backward look. That leaves the three countries of Swaziland, Botswana, and Lesotho unless we count the former British section of French-speaking Cameroun. This is the hard political and economic reality, but if it smells too much of the atlas and safari, let the poet Abioseh Nicol of Sierra Leone set the picture in proper light for us in his poem 'The Meaning of Africa':

> You are not a country, Africa,
> You are a concept,
> Fashioned in our minds, each to each,
> To hide our separate fears,
> To dream our separate dreams.[1]

[1] 'The Meaning of Africa', *A Book of African Verse* (London, Heinemann, 1964).

The dreams we want to explore are those supposedly separate to African poets of English expression as against, I suppose, those by Africans who compose in French, Arabic, Ahmaric, Portuguese, Spanish and in any of the hundreds of original languages of Africa known in imperial parlance as 'the vernacular'. With our field now fairly defined, at least in terms of geography, we find it is not that compact and organic after all, but so vast and varied that not even the best of dreams by the most expansive of poets can cover it all. Probably the one factor, quite apart from that of skin colour, that is common to its entire stretch is the fact that Britain, racing against other European powers, made several colonies of it with the possible exception of Liberia, and in pulling out gracefully or otherwise, has left behind the happy legacy of a common language to such an extent and degree that peoples of these African countries consider the language as much theirs as do the people of New Zealand, Canada, India and indeed Great Britain. The one real difference, perhaps, is the additional possession by them of an alternative tongue—a decided advantage!

It must be emphasized that the colonial experience was by no means peculiar to the peoples of these areas, nor was it a uniform manifestation. Rather the British spoliation process seems to have been haphazard, pragmatic they call it beside the logical French procedure, taking on as it pleased the political agent present on the spot, the character and the lie of the land. Thus, for instance, in the humid countries of West Africa the tiny mosquito (the odes that have been written to it!) would not let the mighty stranger pitch his tent with any degree of permanence, while in East, Central and South Africa with the temperate highlands and prospects of chase, fitting occupation for a squire, the English dug themselves in as gentlemen farmers and settlers. So, if a poet in Gambia and another in Zambia were to write on the colonial experience, which naturally they often do, their points of view, barring the one human, in fact animal, desire to be free, are not likely to coincide in one rigid area of reference, their experience of the event being respectively conditioned as it is by environment and other accidents of nature or history.

Then there is the fantastic variety of ethnic groupings of peoples, 'tribes and clans' as these are called, with all their different languages, their social systems, their customs and conventions of religion, their practice of art, and all that sum total of activities which members of each group have and share in common from birth till death, identifying them from others however closely related. There are hundreds of such human groups, each perhaps as distinct from the other as the Slavs are from the Latin or the Germanic peoples.

If I seem here to place a premium on difference of identity, it is because there is the need to do this so that we do not fall into the popular pastime of indiscriminately lumping together African peoples. The truth is that these differences do exist among the numerous peoples of Africa, forming for each that special cultural make-up and sensibility which any artist anywhere must partake of and be impregnated with before he can bring forth any work of meaning to his people and mankind in general. And the poet in Africa is no different in this respect. Perhaps that was what Janheinz Jahn meant by his 'criteria of culture' which he set up as the one determinant of the work of an author that is African. In other words, a person can be African by birth or race and yet be unable to produce work in either English or French that is of the African experience, with due respect of course to his particular portion of the continent. I suppose this is the one justification for excluding from our field the Roy Campbells for all their contact with Zulu girls breast-feeding their babies in the sun. The point must however not be driven too far if we are to avoid falling over the heady precipice of cultural superiority, racial purity and all that!

To sum up here, poets in Africa writing in English do have 'a language in common' among themselves as indeed *The Times Literary Supplement* admits they do with other English-speaking peoples of the world. But what use each puts the common tool to depends upon the special skill and immediate conditions of his individual person and place. His preoccupation accordingly may be the encounter of the black with the incursive white or it may be ordinary human affections and dislikes, hopes and fears, joys and jobs that are the run of life for adult minds anywhere. After all, an orchestra does not contain the piano alone, overwhelming as can be the harmony or discord from black and white keys. It also has room for several more instruments, strings and woodwind, brass and timpani, if the piece of music it is playing must attain its maximum body.

Now, the often forgotten fact is that several of the African poets writing in English are no different from their French-speaking compatriots in their love for the one theme and tune of 'Africa Lost and Regained'. The French set, assuming the methodical manner of their masters, coined that beautiful word 'negritude' for this grand passion. Our set on the other hand, for all their not being assimilated, must have had a little of the British humbug rubbing off on them for although they bear no labels and belong to no celebrated schools or movements, the very name Africa is 'like a bell to toll' them back to their glorious past of 'tall palm trees', 'cool breezes wafting over pleasant lagoons', 'bare-breasted virgins, and simple trusting men of brains and brawn treacherously lured into slavery abroad' and loss of 'human dignity' at home. Not that this did not happen as the American Malcolm X well reminds us!

We shall call these poets the 'pioneer' poets of Ghana and the 'pilot' poets of Nigeria; first because they were early on the scene and belonged to the vanguard of the fight for political freedom and secondly, for the simple reason that they wrote for newspapers of those names. In this vein Mr Michael Dei-Anang of Ghana gushes over Africa:

> I love the days of long ago,
> Great days of virtuous Chastity,
> When wild men and wilder beasts,
> Kept close company,
> I love Africa as herself—

> Unsophisticated queenly Africa
> That previous pearl of the past.[1]

And similarly Chief Dennis Osadebay of Mid-Western Nigeria who often adopts an apologetic if defiant tone as in his 'Young Africa's Plea':

> Don't preserve my customs
> As some fine curios
> To suit some white historian's tastes.[2]

Of course, the chant, the monotone and the sonority as of incantation of words melting into melody, and therefore requiring to be sung to the cora to 'pass into tradition', as preached and persistently practised by Senghor, are all lacking in this type of poetry. This however was not because our poets were less sincere than their French-speaking contemporaries or less passionate about their love for Africa. Rather, we should accept between the English and French-speaking sets of the forties such distinction as exists between the English poets Shadwell and Dryden. Both men were moved by the events of their times and wrote passionately in the interest of their causes or patrons, but one remains a dull pamphleteer today while the other retains the unmistakable fire of poetry that informed his lines. In this connection, it might be worth our while noting the rather obvious dash of the early English classical style present in this pioneer poetry in English by Africans. Similarly, the *Hymnal Companion* seems to have served as a regular source for models.

The pioneer school of 'Africa, my Africa' did not quite die out with the cool breeze that blew then everywhere through the tall palm trees swaying stately and tall over lagoons in the tropical African sun. Such was their ready stock of vocabulary, phrases and sentiment that a compiler who cared enough could easily have made out of it a dictionary of poetry. But if the pioneer school did not quite go from strength to strength,

---

[1] 'I love the days of long ago', *Poems from Black Africa*, ed. Langston Hughes (Bloomington, Indiana University Press, 1963).

[2] 'Young Africa's Plea', *Africa Sings* (London, Stockwell, 1952).

its new generation of practitioners at least possessed more self-consciousness and better equipment. One or two show considerable technique and sophistication—the former Mabel Imoukhuede, for instance, her hysterics notwithstanding. Conversely, a 'superior' type, very self-righteous in tone, became fashionable, if only briefly, as can be seen in lines like these taken out of *Nigerian Student Verse* published at the then University College of Ibadan:

> What in ancestral days was fear
> In me is grandeur
> What in ages gone was dread
> In me is splendour.[1]

The smug tone of this poem was rivalled only by that of another called 'Superstition' and appearing in the same collection. For both stereotyped pieces I accept personal responsibility for first using them in the college verse magazine *Horn*. The jealous claims of Africa by her pioneer poets in English and the rather snooty public-school-style rejections by later poetasters may be said therefore to represent responses and reactions to the one theme of Mother Africa.

If the theme of loss and rediscovery got hoarse early in the then British West Africa, it found a relatively late start in both East and Central Africa. Perhaps, poetry of that kind follows politics! In Kenya, Uganda and Tanzania, as in the Rhodesias and Nyasaland, not only had the British come and seen, but it seemed then they had also conquered for keeps. Where in West Africa they had tried some 'de-similation' as against the so-called French assimilation, in their Eastern and Central African colonies the policy shame-facedly was one of segregation with a paternal touch for the natives kept in good behaviour under their chiefs by that famous fossilized imperial arrangement termed 'indirect rule'. The process seemed to promote churches more than schools. Thus the area supplies all of Africa's fine crop of saints and martyrs today while showing little of poetry outside Swahili. But the theme is there

[1] *Nigerian Student Verse*, ed. Martin Sanham (Ibadan).

45

all right—of white meeting black and the tragic loss for the latter thereby. J. D. Rubadiri records this feelingly in his 'Stanley Meets Mutesa':

> Such a time of it they had;
> The heat of the day
> The chill of the night
> And the mosquitoes that followed.
> Such was the time and
> They bound for a kingdom.[1]

The Magi of Lancelot Andrews and T. S. Eliot seeking out the new-born Christ have become the explorer Stanley and his commandeered band of porters bringing new dispensation to Mutesa on their way to Livingstone, we presume!

In South Africa, because of the peculiar spoliation of the Bantu peoples and their land, the colour and encounter theme takes on alarming shades. Indeed, it is hard to believe how so much puerile poetry could have come from a people who have produced so much virile prose. My friend Ezekiel Mphahlele, a fine embodiment of this paradox, offers the special debilitating conditions of Apartheid as the excuse. 'They suck up all the energies of the black South African writer' he insists. And he adds that if Apartheid is spur at all to the artist, it leaves him too paralysed to achieve anything of value. Well, is this wholly so? Have some of the best works of art not been created by artists labouring under crippling conditions? Beethoven in his deafness, Milton in his blindness and fall, and (was it) Dostoievsky, imprisoned and facing the firing squad, to drop but a few names, did they not turn disaster into triumph? One would have thought hardship, rather than happiness, played midwife to genius. Perhaps this is the romantic view, considering that the great scientific discoveries and technological developments, since the American Thomas Edison made Big Business of invention, have been made from comfortable chairs and well-endowed laboratories.

Without doubt, Apartheid is the dragon that calls up much of the poetry written by Africans in South Africa, but so real

[1] 'Stanley Meets Mutesa', *A Book of African Verse*, op. cit.

and engulfing is the fire it breathes down over the poets, many of them dare not face the monster squarely. In that process, they turn to several forms of sublimation of the subject; thus the exile theme, the pastoral theme, and the sheer exhibition-ism theme of so much of the verse coming out of the Cape of Good Hope and its hinterland of hate. A few specimens will do for our purpose:

In 'Exile In Nigeria' by Ezekiel Mphahlele, the harmattan:

> Northern Wind
> Sweeping down from the Sahara

does nothing to the poet free for the first time behind—

> windows that were shut so long
> Oh, so long
> in the painful south of the south—[1]

except of course to whip up this marathon piece of panting. Fine emotions the poem has in plenty, and there is no scarcity of fine moments. But on the whole, it remains one raw inchoate mass scoured about by the harmattan wind with sands shored up from 'Down Second Avenue'. Compare this with the surgeon Lenrie Peters savouring Gambia from the septic wards of London in 'Homecoming':

> There at the edge of the town
> Just by the burial ground
> Stands the house without a shadow
> Lived in by new skeletons.
>
> This is all that is left
> To greet us on the home coming
> After we have paced the world
> And longed for returning.[2]

One suspects in the first a missing of the proper medium, for the poet, as everybody knows, wields a powerful prose style.

With Peter Clarke the painter we take leave of the terrible ills rampant in his shanty towns and cities for the idyllic scenes of some countryside.

[1] 'Exile in Nigeria', *Poems from Black Africa*, op. cit.
[2] 'Homecoming', *Modern Poetry from Africa* (London, Penguin, 1963).

> Let's go up to the hillside today
> to play, to play
> to play—[1]

so goes the invitation in his 'Play Song'. After that we are drifting among 'five gleaming crows' in 'In Air', or dissolving 'in ecstasy' with his 'Young Shepherd Bathing His Feet'— a title very reminiscent of Monet! Such a pastoral burst in a prospect very bleak can be most welcome.

Not so the professional exhibitionism abundant in verses by Bloke Modisane:

> God
> glad I'm black;
> pitch-forking devil black:
> black, black, black—[2]

declares the poet in 'Blue black' to all the world. In the companion piece 'Black blue', riddled with the same parallel phrasing, he tries a subtle variation to the theme:

> the blues is the black o' the face,
> I said: black is the blues' face;
> It's black in the mornin'
> beige in the sun;
> and blue black all night long.[3]

This becomes in 'Lonely', I suppose, the wail of a flute in duet with a screaming saxophone:

> I talk to myself when I write,
> shout and scream to myself,
> then to myself
> scream and shout:[4]

With this type of poetry it is not too uncharitable to say its complete repertoire consists of the following words and concepts: 'black' and 'blue(s)', 'scream' and 'shout', with 'loneliness' in all its forms closing the litany. It is the nearest thing

---

[1] 'Play Song', *Poems from Black Africa*, op. cit.

[2] 'Blue black', ibid.

[3] 'Black blue', ibid.

[4] 'Lonely', *Modern Poetry from Africa*, op. cit.

in Africa to American Negro folk poetry—which is not surprising, for the situations are similar. The one difference however is that in America the black man will always remain a minority while in South Africa he can actually achieve the position of power. Otherwise, he is the same man dehumanized by whites, uprooted from what they are the first to label 'tribal life', and flaunting in the face of other blacks and Africans, who know nothing of the four temperate seasons, the great fact of 'the urban civilization' to which they proudly belong.

In general, poets of this class possess an ambivalent attitude to their own kin and skin that can best be described in these words by their big brother Langston Hughes: 'Some of the younger poets are completely lacking in negritude—several of the fashionable beatnik side—but not bad in that genre. Some quite dark in colour, but one can't tell their writing from whites —which maybe is what integration is supposed to do: erase the colour line from waiting-rooms to writing. Do you reckon?' The question was for his friend Rosey Poole who answered thus, all faithfully recorded in her anthology *Beyond the Blues*: 'A sound amount of negritude saves the Negro from wanting to "pass" or forget, and from going Black Moslem'. Is it surprising then the flagellated black skin has become a fine fetish like the thorn-and-nail marks of the man who died on the cross?

There is, however, some strenuous striving going on at the same time to forge out of the confusion and conflict afflicting a country like South Africa what my friend Richard Rive calls 'a higher synthesis of being', and I use the word 'forge' advisedly. Rive's tone in 'Where the Rainbow Ends' inclines to the pedagogic, but true teacher that he is, he will stick out his neck to lecture us all to sanity in lines such as these:

> There's no such tune as a black tune;
> There's no such tune as a white tune;
> There's only music, brother;
> And it's music we are going to sing;
> Where the rainbow ends.[1]

[1] 'Where the Rainbow Ends', *Poems from Black Africa*, op. cit.

Much more successful still is Joseph Kariuki in 'Come Away, My Love,' putting flesh and blood inside the dress that is colour:

> The candle-light throws
> Two dark shadows on the wall
> Which merge into one as I close beside you.
> When at last the lights are out,
> And I feel your hand in mine,
> Two human breaths join in one,
> And the piano weaves
> Its unchallenged harmony.[1]

In *Sirens, Knuckles, Boots*, a volume of poetry published by Mbari in Nigeria, Dennis Brutus, actually then on the run from Verwoerd's police who later shot him down, succeeds to a considerable extent in transforming life direct into art. Poetry here is servant to politics. Something of the troubadour that he proclaims himself to be, Brutus cuts a tough figure of great bravura, with quite a brutal Elizabethan hold on words, and a strong smell for all the right sentiments to stir the would-be crusader safe in his liberal seat somewhere in Europe and America. Reading the work of Dennis Brutus, much of it re-modelled rhetoric, one comes back to that old excuse by Mphahlele that certain situations like those in South Africa really are too paralysing for words. Perhaps—for what does one do to a dog holding up a mauled paw? A child in a fit of convulsion? Dennis Brutus in his book is a man battering his head against the bars of a cage in which he and his kind are undoubtedly held down by a devilish gaoler. The sight is terrible enough, but one gets the feeling sometimes, a wicked one no doubt, that a little less shouting and more silence and mime might not only make for manly dignity but also command attempts at rescue and action. That is the ram's one lesson to man when trussed up by man. In this way, what is truly tragic will not become mere melodrama—overdrawn, posturing, and tear-jerking.

---

[1] 'Come Away, My Love,' *Modern Poetry from Africa*, op. cit.

Unfortunately, I find that this banner-headline approach intrudes right from the title piece of an otherwise valuable volume:

> The sounds begin again;
> the siren in the night
> the thunder at the door
> the shriek of nerves in pain.
>
> Then the keening crescendo
> Of faces split by pain
> the wordless, endless wait
> Only the unfree know
>
> Importunate as rain
> the wraiths exhale their woe
> over the sirens, knuckles, boots;
> my sounds begin again.[1]

A poem like this, however moving, resurrects the old ghost first raised by T. S. Eliot over *Hamlet*—I mean 'objective correlative'.

Comments like mine here will naturally provoke angry retorts to the effect that they stem not so much from ignorance of the facts and indifference to the suffering of fellow human beings as from an annoying habit of mind that will want to ask, for instance, what effort at self-help the victims are themselves making and what the drink and sex inclinations of their leaders are like. I admit a good number of people in West Africa, particularly in Nigeria, not necessarily poets, might well plead guilty to the charge. The educated West African may have been 'corrupted' by contact with whites, but unlike Africans in east, central or southern Africa, he was never really dispossessed, shunted into shanty towns and native reserves, nor forced out into the wilderness, at best an exile carrying 'the pageant of his bleeding heart', more often a beggar flailing for help with the great disability of colour. Rather he has acquired as much of the European mode and outfit put out for sale, and with some jockeying has sunk into his seat in a civil

[1] *Sirens, Knuckles, Boots* (Ibadan, Mbari, 1963).

set-up already in full motion and geared, we hope, to improving the lot of every citizen. This, I suppose, would be the normal situation in all states where members of one sector do not expend all their energies and lives fighting to free themselves from oppression and slavery at the hands of the majority or an armed gang of fascists.

The great complication, perhaps, for the West African élite brought up in a system not quite British is that he swims in a stream of double currents, one traditional, the other modern. These currents do not run completely parallel; in fact, they often are in conflict. Accordingly, you are likely to find him at church or mosque in the morning and in the evening taking a title at home that carries with it sacrifice of some sort to his ancestors and community gods. In the same manner, a man, however 'detribalized' and successful in his city career and profession, will not outgrow the most backward member of his family. By family here we do not mean husband, wife and their children, but the full blooded set-up of the so-called 'extended family' counted down to the last remembered cousin. Within this range of relationship whoever has must take care of the have-not. Often, this means the 'educated' member, better still if he occupies a responsible appointment known by everybody as 'oyinbo post', that is, 'white man's post'. All this, in my belief, puts the West African élite in the peculiar position of being 'modern' and 'traditional' at one and the same time, making him a citizen of two worlds.

That was a long parenthesis, but I took the liberty of drawing it to set in proper frame themes that appear to me to engage our next group of poets, nearly all of them from West Africa. Public gestures, programmes and matters of political propaganda and slogan do not seem to preoccupy their minds, excepting some of them, mostly from Ghana where things, art not excluded, are of course more organized. Quite evident too is an awareness of the conditions of human existence as known to each personally. Following from this, perhaps, is their tacit acceptance, whether in pride or in humility, of the fact that a poem summoned to life by a committee of citizens,

however revolutionary, is more likely to be the hotchpotch
and doggerel that many national anthems are, than a genuine
work of art. And a good number of these poets take themselves
pretty seriously in the belief, I suppose, that as Professor I. A.
Richards and Dr F. R. Leavis put it, the poet 'is the point at
which the growth of the mind shows itself', being poised so to
speak 'at the most conscious point of the race in his
time'.

The Russian Professor Galperina, seeking advice on an
anthology of Nigerian poetry she is compiling, asked me in
Moscow how Wole Soyinka, the poet of 'Telephone Conversation', could write his poem 'Requiem'. Just as it is possible for
a man to laugh on one occasion and cry on another, had been
my answer. I should like to add here that such sophistication
and range are possible only after a poet has attained with his
public the position described above.

'Telephone Conversation' is a dramatic distillation of that
regular vignette of house-hunting that only dogs, children and
the coloured know in London—

> Caught I was, foully
> 'HOW DARK?' . . . I had not misheard . . .
>   'ARE YOU LIGHT
> OR VERY DARK' Button B. Button A. Stench
>
> Of rancid breath of public hide-and-speak
> Red booth. Red pillar-box. Red double-tiered
> Omnibus squelching tar. It *was* real! Shamed
>
> By ill-mannered silence, surrender
> Pushed dumbfoundment to beg simplification
> Considerate she was, varying the emphasis—
> 'ARE YOU DARK? OR VERY LIGHT?' Revelation came.[1]

Revelation of a rather slow-fuse kind, one is tempted to say.
Out of 'Requiem', section six, comes the following:

> This cup I bore, redeem
> When yearning splice
> The thorn branch.

[1] 'Telephone Conversation', *Modern Poetry from Africa*, op. cit.

This earth I pour outward to
Your cry, tend it. It knows full
Worship of the plough

Lest burning follow breath, learn
This air was tempered in wild
Cadences of fire.[1]

Now, one poem is as protest as any 'colour' piece can be, and the other as agonized as the original display by Dylan Thomas. But each realizes a concreteness, immediate and meaningful, that is possible only from a personal, diligent hammering out of the molten material out of which poetry is moulded. A poet equipped like this will handle any stuff that catches his imagination, be it ripening corn as in Soyinka's very English poem 'Season', 'a child born to die' as in his 'Abiku', or an animal run over at dawn by a motorist as in his 'Death in the Dawn'.

Of the same order is Gabriel Okara, a real poet. His is an inward concern, the 'mystic' 'inside', to use his own words. This concern with the self, the soul, runs through all his work, and it is realized by the poet in terms and images of objects and phenomena that most impinge upon his conscious. Snowflakes, a piano, drums, social airs, an aladura or beachside prophet, a river, a stork, a girl too distant to possess, these are what make Okara spark.

The mystic drum beat in my inside
and fishes danced in the rivers
and men and women danced on land
to the rhythm of my drum

But standing behind a tree
with leaves around her waist
she only smiled with a shake of her head.[2]

In these lines from 'The Mystic Drum' the fatal woman of John Keats is not quite hidden from sight as is the Wordsworthian animal breath and exhiliration of 'Piano and Drums'. But both poems are definitely Gabriel Okara, who is no shallow

[1] 'Requiem', *Modern Poetry from Africa*, op. cit.
[2] 'The Mystic Drum', ibid.

sheet of water but a real chameleon figure standing fast in his reflection of the outside world.

Were Okara not an undisputed artist, he could easily fall among the 'pioneer' and 'pilot' poets we spoke of earlier. The tall palm trees, the jungle drums, the innocent virgins, the mystic rhythms, the dark flesh and the old wish not to lose face in a double sense within the alien crowd and clash of so many colours washing in from outside are all well-worn wares of that otherwise respectable house. But in the gifted hands of Okara they become articles of original style and lasting worth. So far, the one crack known to me in Okara's short production line has been his long poem, 'The Fishermen's Invocation'. This, like most other attempts by poets to erect fitting mansions to their names, appears to me a real disaster.

Christopher Okigbo, also from Nigeria, is a different performer entirely. He has been published by Mbari in two slender volumes already. But in these and subsequent poems he himself says his one theme has been a combination of the processes of creation and self-purification. The invocation to *Heavensgate* sets the tone of what appears a very free admixture of Christianity and animism:

> Before you, mother Idoto,
> naked I stand,
> before your watery presence,
> a prodigal,
>
> leaning on an oilbean,
> lost in your legend . . .
>
> Under your power wait I
>   on barefoot,
> Watchman for the watchword
>   at heavensgate;
>
> Out of the depths my cry
> give ear and hearken.[1]

There is a quality to this I have heard some dismiss as precious and contrived. But listen to this from the second volume, *Limits*:

[1] *Heavensgate* (Ibadan, Mbari, 1962).

> Bright
> With the armpit dazzle of a lioness,
> she answers,
> wearing white light about her;
> and the waves escort her,
> my lioness,
> crowned with moonlight
>
> So brief her presence—
> match-flare in wind's breath—
> so brief with mirrors around me.
>
> Downward . . .
> the waves distil her:
> Gold crop
> Sinking ungathered.
> Watermaid of the salt emptiness,
> grown are the ears of the secret.[1]

I notice I used the word 'listen' in connection with the above poem. I think it is an apt word with Christopher Okigbo. Listen, and you will hear fine glass breaking on highly polished floor, the catch of breath, the patter of tiny feet; all converging to one point—but perhaps I am reading all this into the poet! Yet, listen again, and now certainly you can recognize the several grains to the glass dazzling scattered in the light. Or if we may mix metaphors, the strands and threads, the woofs and wefts of the fine dress worn with such assurance. The bright aura and dazzle, the armpit, the lioness, the white light, the waves as escort, the crown and moonlight, the transcience of the maid like 'match-flare in the wind's breath', the mirrors and gold crop all constitute an apparatus completely taken from Pound's Cantos 4 and 106 where the 'downward' movement here really was 'upward', and the wind that of the King.

These poems are each carefully scored out like a musical piece. Some sections in fact require playing to the flute, although to what tune the poet, like Senghor with his cora, does not say. Together, they confirm to my mind the possession by the poet of a rare gift of literary imagination. This operates

---

[1] *Limits* (Ibadan, Mbari, 1964).

by a process I will not call predatory, as that suggests vampires and parasites; rather it seizes upon what attracts it and distils therefrom, without destroying the original, a fresh artefact. A later work, 'Silences', slight as it is, presents a remarkable mosaic of world literature, music and painting. It is a stimulating game detecting within it the originals and borrowed bits. It becomes even more exciting since this was a game the poet delighted in playing against himself.

This survey, incomplete as it is, would be even less complete if I failed to drop a comment or two on the poetic performance in places like Ghana and elsewhere. I should like to quote Gerald Moore and Ulli Beier on this: 'It is interesting to see the use which has been made of vernacular poetry by two of these English-speaking poets, George Awoonor-Williams of Ghana and Mazisi Kunene of South Africa. Both have understood and assimilated the cryptic, rather oracular quality of much vernacular imagery. This has given both freshness and weight to their language. Both incidentally come from areas where a great deal of fine vernacular poetry has been collected, Eweland and Zululand.'[1] Now theirs may well be called a concern and quest for the wisdom and wealth of their fathers. Dzogbese Lisa in 'Songs of Sorrow' by Awoonor-Williams undoubtedly is the same divinity that Melville and Frances Herskovits found hedging destiny in Dahomey, and in the lament by the old Ashanti warrior of his 'Song of War' we have a whole age summoned up to view.

In this search for the wisdom and wealth of the past we may join other Ghanaians like Efua Sutherland and Joe de Graft, who are willing to reach for truth without damning the evidence to uphold set theories or beliefs. This is no easy task, for in a mission like theirs it is easier to compromise in the interest of old images and new idols than to be flippant or cynical. De Graft and Sutherland, when I ran into them in Accra two years ago on my way to New York, were both engaged in an exciting experiment. This appeared to me one

---

[1] Introduction to *Modern Poetry from Africa*, op. cit.

of exploiting to the full on the stage, in a poetic manner, the heroic and imaginative stories from Ghana's history and ancient lore. One attempt at such a recreation for the theatre, I remember well, appeared first in *Okyeame*, the journal of the Ghana Union of Writers or some such body. The pity, however, was that it was as dead as *Gorboduc*—particularly in the style which was blank verse straight and proper!

The Ghanaian philosopher Willie Abraham in his controversial book *The Mind of Africa* throws some light upon the issue. 'Our interest in our own cultures is not historical or archaeological, but directed towards the future', he says on the subject of ideology and society. 'It helps importantly in solving the question not what Africans were like, but how we can make the best of our present human resources, which are largely traditional.'[1] Otherwise, we fall into all the traps and escape hatches that negritude for all its fine services offers the unwary, like the black of the earth being all soul and music and the whites all intellect and machine. We shall therefore go some way with Kwesi Brew when in 'The Search' he says of the past:

> So look not for wisdom
> And guidance
> In their speech, my beloved.
> Let the same fire
> Which chastened their tongues
> Into silence,
> Teach us—teach us[2]

In another minute, let us hope we too shall have learnt silence!

About my own preoccupation in poetry I have chosen to keep quiet not from any sense of modesty, which is often false, but from a simple professional stand. I have already made them the subject of a small introductory essay for a volume of my selected poems which Longman is publishing. If you have had the singular patience to sit through this paper, I have no fears you will certainly call for the other! In the meantime,

[1] *The Mind of Africa* (London, Weidenfeld and Nicholson, 1962).

[2] 'The Search', *Shadows of Laughter* (London, Longman, 1968).

may I give some advice to some of those who of late have been doing brisk business collecting and promoting anthologies of poems from Africa on both sides of the Atlantic. Easily in the lead is my old friend Langston Hughes. In *Poems from Black Africa* published by Indiana University Press in 1963, Langston makes the following pronouncement: 'Contemporary young African intellectuals, some of whom have but lately come home from Cambridge or the Sorbonne, are not unlike young writers elsewhere. They have read Auden and Spender and Eliot, Mauriac, Jacques Prévert and perhaps Brecht. Lagos, Accra or Dakar are no longer weeks away from Europe. In fact, from the heart of Africa to Paris or London by jet is now only a matter of hours. Not that all African writers have travelled abroad. But the bookshops in Africa's major cities today are fairly well stocked.' Now this is the kind of double-take and clever talk around the obvious that his compatriot James Baldwin does so well—especially in *The Fire Next Time*.

But listen to Langston again: 'Whatever their influences may be, local or foreign, there are sensitive and exciting poets in black Africa now.' Accordingly, he goes on to pack his anthology with prodigies and pieces that on their present showing will not find space at home even on the pages of a Sunday paper. So that when the editor goes on to state 'Meanwhile, it walks with grace and already is beginning to achieve an individuality quite its own'—one wonders whether he has, for some purpose known only to himself put on blinkers or whether it is just that he cannot discriminate between the wren and the hen.

That is not all. Langston Hughes adopts in his anthology a proportional representation approach as if poetry were politics and every country in Africa a constituency to be equally represented. Furthermore, he not only re-arranges lines and rewrites whole poems as he does with two pieces of mine but he also appears to make verses out of short stories and novels like those by Peter Abrahams. With a presentation like that, one can well understand why Langston, in the course of a six-line biographical note on the poet J. P. Clark, made so much of the fact that he 'bears three tiny cast marks beside his eyes and four on each cheek, as is the custom of his tribe'. Well, poets in Africa of English and indeed of whatever expression might be many of the things Langston Hughes dwells on in his folksy-talky black anthology: some in fact are legislators, some professional men, and quite a few must be cannibals. But I hope they are not liars as well with their calling and vocation; for then they should really deserve kicking out of their respective republics, as Plato enjoined some two thousand years ago, and my hosts in Moscow undoubtedly practise at every season of the revolution.

3: The communication line between poet and public

Nigeria possesses two traditions of poetry—poetry of the 'oral tradition' which the various Nigerian peoples have always practised according to their own needs and conventions, and poetry of the 'literate tradition', a product of the colonial experience that Nigerians have all suffered together. Of this latter, which is our concern here, there are again two separate traditions, one belonging to the generation that reached its prime in the thirties and forties, and the other to the present generation of poets now fully realizing itself. This is not just a distinction in time. Between the groups there exist definite differences, principally in the matter of performance and the public each enjoys. Indeed our primary objective here is to prove that in the development of poetry of the literate kind in Nigeria there ran at one time a direct line of communication between poet and public, a link that practically disappears between the later poets and the public, and is only now being studiously cultivated for reasons not completely literary. This is the kind of link that Sir Herbert Grierson in his inaugural lecture at Edinburgh more than half a century ago elaborated for English literature under the title *The Background of English Literature*.[1]

The case as outlined then for English literature holds good today for Nigerian poetry written down in English. First, 'the most ordinary speaker or penny-a-liner and the greatest poet are alike linked to their audience by certain media of which the first is the language they use. English journalist and English poet use the English language because they are writing for

---

[1] *The Background of English Literature and other essays* (London, Penguin, 1925. Reprinted 1962).

English-speaking people, though there may be all the difference in the world in the degree of precision and delicacy with which they use that language.' Secondly, 'the speaker and writer is connected with his audience by other links as well as that of a common language—by a body of common knowledge and feeling to which he may make direct or indirect allusion confident that he will be understood, and not only this, but more or less accurately aware of the effect which the allusion will produce. He knows roughly what his audience knows, and what are their prejudices. A people is made one, less by community of blood than by a common tradition.' Thirdly, the Classical and Biblical 'are the two most important vistas in the background of (English) literature until, at any rate, very recent days—literature and history to which a poet might refer with some confidence of being understood, and further, a certain feeling towards which of interest, respect, or reverence was a tie that connected him with his audience, a feeling on which he could count to give values to his picture'. The fourth point is that for one reason or another, 'these days are past. Long threatened and slowly modified, our traditional education has ... rapidly disintegrated ... Now if a poet wishes to give his work a literary background, if he is one of those whose inspiration is caught from books, whose imagination loves strange civilizations and scenery remote in time or space, then he writes necessarily for a limited audience, and to that extent he creates his own background from himself'.

But the more general result, the most characteristic tendency of recent poetry, has been to eliminate any conscious reference to a literary background altogether, to give poetry a setting not of literature and tradition but of nature and actuality.'[1]

That of course covers the whole long sweep of English literature from Chaucer to almost our own day. With the 'moderns' Hopkins, Yeats, Eliot and Pound we come to a traumatic break in the line of communication that prevailed

[1] Ibid.

all along between poet and public in England. The course of Nigerian poetry written down in English, admittedly a very short one, shows a line of contact and break quite similar to that drawn above by Grierson. At one extreme end of the line is a poet like Chief Dennis Osadebay whose compeers are Dr Nnamdi Azikiwe, Mr A. K. Blankson, Mr Christopher Okejie and Chief Kola Balogun, and at the other a poet like Mr Christopher Okigbo, with little or no communication between both poets.

But one or two modifications must be made in our adoption of the Grierson formula. It is not that the Bible and the Classics are necessarily the main vistas upon which earlier Nigerian poetry in English as distinct from the later poetry opens. Nor is it that when such vistas actually feature in one, are they for that reason absent in the other. Indeed, the evidence may very well be the reverse! What must be remembered is that during the first half of the development of Nigerian poetry in English there was a union of language and feeling between the poet and the public. In the latter half, probably as a result of changes in education and outlook, poets and people no longer seem to share that one language and viewpoint to life, either on the personal or national level.

Chief Dennis Osadebay's *Africa Sings* was published by the author himself in 1952. It is a collection of some hundred poems written 'between 1930 and 1950, some in Nigeria, some at sea and others in England'. All of them first appeared 'in Nigerian, British and Indian papers and magazines, notably the *Nigerian Daily Times, Daily Service, Comet, Eastern Mail, West African Pilot, Empire,* and *Aryan*'.[1]

A single vista informs these poems, that of one man's first awakening to a vision of himself and his environment. To use the poet's own words again: 'The theme running throughout the book is the urge in the heart of the African to be free and the desire that African nations should take their rightful places in the world family of free nations. Africa sings, not only songs

[1] *Africa Sings* (London, Stockwell, 1952).

63

of love and joy, but also touching lamentations flowing from the soul of teeming millions, yearning, pleading, struggling, waiting.' Accordingly, there abound in the collection laments, pleas, explanations, resolves and thanks by Young Africa, a prototype character that is the personification of all nationalist suffering and aspiration on the continent and beyond. Closely connected with this strain are the odes, making up more than a third of the volume, addressed to assorted subjects and persons. The roll-call ranges from workers, union leaders, priests and political leaders, including Hitler and Mussolini, to the poet's old school, his adopted towns, a Yaba doctor who cured him of a malarial attack, and to the River Niger, the Palm Tree, and his Raleigh Cycle. Obviously, these are subjects very close to the poet's consciousness, although others, especially the foreigner and expatriate overlord of that time, might not hold them dear:

> Don't preserve my customs
> As some fine curios
> To suit some white historian's tastes.
> There's nothing artificial
> That beats the natural way,
> In culture and ideals of life.[1]

Allied to this new claim and pride for properties, old and indigenous to Africa, is the bold stake constantly made by the poet on the intellectual wealth of Europe:

> Let me play with the white man's ways,
> Let me work with the black man's brains,
> Let my affairs themselves sort out
> Then in sweet rebirth
> I'll rise a better man,
> Not ashamed to face the world.[2]

Again and again he expresses the same resolve:

> On library doors
> I'll knock aloud and gain entrance,

---

[1] 'Young Africa's Plea', *Africa Sings*, op. cit.
[2] Ibid.

> Of the strength
> Of nations past and present and will read.
> I'll brush the dust from ancient scrolls
> And drinking deep of the Pyrrhean stream,
> Will go forward and do and dare.[1]

Besides this overall feeling of personal and national consciousness, the other property immediately noticeable in this poetry is the language. The stock of words, the syntactic constructions, the well-worn imagery are of the kind to reach at once the regular readership of the newspapers which first featured these poems. Then there are the inversions taken for obvious poetic effects, the sedulous rhymes, the recurrent epithets, the clichés and echoes, and the apostrophizing habits all of which evoke a ready response in an audience familiar with their popular proverbial lines taken from Pope, Gray and the hymn-makers Isaac Watts, William Cowper and the Wesley brothers.

The poet wants no material wealth, and echoing St Peter, announces boldly 'not gold not silver do I crave'. But he must win for himself the Golden Fleece of education, the one treasure that would make Young Africa the co-equal of Europe and free him of political and mental bondage:

> I do not crave for riches
> Nor worldly pomp and power;
> I ask for God's free air
> And shelter from the elements;
> Give me these rights of man;
> The right to think my Thoughts,
> The right to say my views,
> The right to stand erect.[2]

These are sentiments spelling out a vision of life fully shared by poet and public alike in the Nigeria of Herbert Macaulay and Dr Nnamdi Azikiwe.

It may also be said that the poet at this point of the development of a written poetry in Nigeria was actually part and

---

[1] 'Young Africa's Resolve', *Africa Sings*, op. cit.
[2] 'My Ambition', ibid.

parcel of a people and generation only then taking their first firm grip on a foreign tongue that for better or worse had become for their countrymen the language of prestige, business, and education. He had therefore to master the language first, a difficult task for a junior customs officer just freshly matriculated, before working experiments with it. This is not to say that the later poets have had a shorter cut to learning English and writing poetry. Rather they may be said to have been born into a tradition of speech already accepted and aspired to by all. Therefore the atmosphere for learning would be less hostile and the tensions easier on the nerves. Furthermore, Nigerian poets of today have had a longer time to study in depth both language and medium, enjoying the additional benefit of a wider choice of practice and models. In this context, credit must be given Chief Dennis Osadebay who really is a pioneer poet celebrating the rising sun of his people. The realistic ring of voice he obtains in *Blackman Trouble* by a bold use of pidgin is therefore remarkable:

> I no get gun, I no get bomb,
> I no fit fight no more;
> You bring your cross and make me dumb
> My heart get plenty sore.
> You tell me close my eyes
> Your brother thief my land away.[1]

Style and tone here sound much more convincing than Mr Frank Aig-Imoukhuede, almost twenty years after, achieves in the much admired *One Man One Wife*. Furthermore, Chief Osadebay well demonstrates here that pidgin, far from being confined to humorous writing, possesses the potential for registering a wide range of the human mind, pathos included.

The chain of instant communication, so strong between Chief Osadebay and his audience, breaks almost defiantly, in the hands of Mr Christopher Okigbo. With him feeling and language are no longer the common property of poet and public. 'I don't read my poetry to non-poets!' he told a conference of writers at Kampala in 1962. But perhaps we should

[1] 'Blackman Trouble', ibid.

listen to him through his acknowledged master and model Ezra Pound. 'If we never write anything save what is already understood', the master says in *Thrones*, 'the field of understanding will never be extended. One demands the right, now and again, to write for a few people with special interests and whose curiosity reaches into greater detail'.[1]

> DUMB-BELLS outside the gates
> In hollow seascapes without memory, we carry
> Each of us an urn of native
> Earth, a double handful anciently gathered.
> And by salt mouths by yellow
> Sand banks sprinkled with memories spread
> To the nightairs our silence,
> Suffused in this fragrance of divers melodies:
> This is our swan song
> This is our senses' stillness:
> For we carry in our world that flourishes
> Our worlds that have failed . . .
> This is the sigh of our spirits:
> For unseen shadows like long-fingered winds
> Pluck from our strings
> This shriek—the music of the firmament.

What kind of audience hears this music? For, to quote Ezra Pound once more, 'Here, surely, is a refinement of language'. Mr Okigbo himself in his earlier poem 'Limits' acknowledges this limitation or complete lack of listeners, for there the poet is—

> Tongue-tied without name or audience,
> Making harmony among the branches.[2]

Even in the later piece *Lament for a suite of long-drums and seven tusks* where Mr Okigbo consciously draws upon the Yoruba Oriki and the tradition of Ibo praise poetry, both ancient forms of art establishing immediate contact between artist and audience, there is the same apparent break in communication between poet and public. Like Palinurus, the lost leader

---

[1] *Thrones* (London, Faber, 1960).
[2] *Limits* (Ibadan, Mbaru, 1964).

he sings of, the poet here seems all 'alone in a hot prison' keeping at best 'the dead sea awake with nightsong'. Consequently, when the drums beat out 'on the orange yellow myth of the sands of exile',

> Long-drums dis-
> Jointed, and with bleeding tendons
> Like tarantulas
> Emptied of their bitterest poisons

the effect upon the audience that should be participating in an urgent experience is:

> like a dead letter unanswered,
> Our rococo
> Choir of insects is null
> Cacophony
> And void as a debt summons served
> On a bankrupt—

although:

> the antiphony, still clamorous
> In tremolo,
> Like an afternoon, for shadows;
> And the winds
> the distant seven cannons invite us
> To a sonorous
> Ishthar's lament for Tammuz.[1]

This is poetry that proceeds by a technique different from the early simple statements and sentiments of Chief Dennis Osadebay. Overall movement or logistics, as Mr Okigbo himself calls it, is gained here by the accumulated utterance, often separated by parenthesis and then woven together again by use of the old narrative 'and', so that the phrasing sounds on the whole fragmentary, while the frequent repetitions, as if for breath, as well as the increasingly latinate and exotic words and names, make for a total effect that at best attains musicality and at worst prolixity.

Such language is not for sharing with the general public.

---

[1] *Lament for a suite of long-drums and seven tusks*, *Transition* No. 18.

Nor is the feeling that generates it; that too is very private. In the words of Grierson we may say of a poet like this that his 'inspiration is caught from books'. And his 'imagination loves strange civilizations and scenery remote in time or space' to such an extent 'he writes necessarily for a limited audience' since the poet 'creates his own background from himself'. As a matter of fact, Okigbo's *Lament for a suite of long-drums and seven tusks* recalls the Babylonian hymn *Lament of the Flutes for Tammuz*, sung at the secret rites of Adonis in Syria:

> At his vanishing away she lifts up a lament,
> 'Oh my child!' at his vanishing away she lifts up a lament;
> 'My Damu!' at his vanishing away she lifts up a lament.
> 'My enchanter and priest!' at his vanishing away she lifts up a
> lament,
> At the shining cedar, rooted in a spacious place,
> In Eanna, above and below, she lifts up a lament.
> Like the lament that a house lifts up for its master, lifts she up a
> lament,
> Like the lament that a city lifts up for its lord, lifts she up a
> lament,
> Her lament is the lament for a herb that grows not in the bed,
> Her lament is the lament for the corn that grows not in the ear,
> Her chamber is a possession that brings not forth a possession,
> A weary woman, a weary child, forspent.
> Her lament is for a great river, where no willows grow,
> Her lament is for a field, where corn and herbs grow not.
> Her lament is for a pool, where fishes grow not.
> Her lament is for a thicket of reeds, where no reeds grow.
> Her lament is for woods, where tamarisks grow not.
> Her lament is for a wilderness where no cypresses (?) grow.
> Her lament is for the depth of a garden of trees, where honey and
> wine grow not.
> Her lament is for meadows, where no plants grow.
> Her lament is for a palace, where length of life grows not.

The distancing achieved here by Okigbo is of course relative, that is, the poem is obscure in inverse proportion with the ignorance of the reader vis-à-vis the poet. In other words, only the reader who possesses a field of reference corresponding in area to that evoked by this literary imagination will appreciate at once and fully the themes and allusions of this brand of poetry. But for many readers, this is asking a lot, and among the few who claim to understand and share with the poet his experience there is often disagreement. Mr O. R. Dathorne, for example, in a review of *Limits* in *Black Orpheus* Vol 1 No 15, pontificates: '*Silences*, which appeared in *Transition* 8 is the liturgy of the intending initiates who "camp in a convent in the open" and *Limits*, exploring the penetralia of the unconscious state of non-being, narrates the progress towards nirvana'; while Mr Paul Theroux in his essay 'Six Poets', reprinted in *Introduction to African Literature*, edited by Ulli Beier, is convinced that all Okigbo's poetry 'can be considered from the point of view of all theologies, mythologies—each yields an interpretation'.[1] An omnipresent all-inclusive vista like this will of course include the subordinate ones of the Classics and the Bible which indeed are significant ones for Mr Okigbo.

Claims like these must emanate from true believers. Without being sceptical, it may safely be said that, seen against the performance and philosophy of Chief Dennis Osadebay, gone here are the public statements, the identification of personal problems with the struggles and aspirations of divers peoples just beginning then to recognize themselves as of a corporate body with one country, one destiny, one God. In this process Nigerian poetry has moved from the pages of daily newspapers, from the soapbox and platform of popular political meetings, held in cinema halls and the open market-place, to the private study of the individual and the exlusive confines of senior common-rooms.

In between these two extreme points and within the second segment of the national graph come Mr Okigbo's contemporaries like Mr Gabriel Okara and Mr Wole Soyinka, each in his own individual position. By our fourth rider, again in the words of Grierson, these poets in their performance and

[1] *Introduction to African Literature* (London, Longmans, 1967).

language 'give poetry a setting not of literature and tradition but of nature and actuality'. In so doing each carries a measure of communication, complete or partial, commensurate with the degree of validity successfully realized by him in the treatment of a particular subject. It is this concern for 'nature and actuality' that provides the personal link between each and his audience, a much wider one than Mr Okigbo enjoys, if at the same time much narrower than Chief Osadebay's. The drums, pianos, changeling girl as well as storks and snows of Mr Okara are subjects directly recognizable to his audience. Similarly, the abiku, the accident-prone traveller and London 'digs' hunter of Mr Soyinka, and I suppose my own night-sleeper, Agbor dancer, Fulani cattle, Ibadan and other evocations of that kind. These are natural concrete subjects realized for the reader in a personal memorable way by each poet in the unconscious hope of adding some fresh dimension to life.

Mr Okara, who of this group of poets occupies a position perhaps closest to Chief Osadebay's in the line of communication, provides in 'One Night at Victoria Beach' probably the best evidence demonstrating the difference between earlier and later Nigerian poetry written in English:

> The wind comes rushing from the sea,
> the waves curling like mambas strike
> the sands and recoiling hiss in rage
> washing the Aladuras' feet pressing hard
> on the sand and with eyes fixed hard
> on what only hearts can see, they shouting
> pray, the Aladuras pray; and coming
> from booths behind, compelling highlife
> forces ears; and car lights startle pairs
> arm in arm passing washer-words back
> and forth like haggling sellers and buyers—[1]

Now compare this with 'Thoughts at the Victoria Beach: Lagos' by Chief Osadebay:

> The Waters stretched from the tropic shores
> And seemed to kiss the sunlit skies afar;

[1] 'One Night at Victoria Beach', *Modern Poetry from Africa*, op. cit.

The waves riding in Majesty,
Glided to and fro like lords of the silvery bar.
The off washed sands gave forth a smile
To beautify the sphere and heaven extol;
The noble palm and mangrove trees
Stood with their heads aloft as the waters roll.
Poor mortals—birds and beasts and men—
Ran here and there in vain attempt to keep
Their lives from the quenching winds of death,
And sought in vain to solve the mysteries deep.[1]

Both poems, though on the same subject, are worlds apart in language and attitude. The wind, waves, and sand of Mr Okara carry all the menace, urgency and movement of the snake; in the hands of Chief Osadebay they remain static, decorative motifs as those upon any painting from Nigeria's palm tree-and-lagoon school. In the composite scene of priests in prayer, a pub dinning with highlife music, a pair of lovers caught haggling like the fisherwomen on the beach, Mr Okara conjures up with a few strokes the changeless fair of human wishes. Here wares, precious and worthless, lie cheek by jowl, indistinguishable from one another. The serious and the comic are close neighbours, and in the claims and counter-claims of each for attention, there is no telling who is the central figure to the drama of life.

This human interest is hardly realized in concrete terms in the Osadebay poem. There, instead of an active drama of flux, we are fobbed off with a tableau of poor mortals running 'to keep their lives from the quenching winds of death'. And they stop at the same time to seek 'in vain to solve the mysteries deep'. Later, the poet says:

My mind rummaged the Universe
In search of why's and wherefores of life.[2]

In that uncanny quest he discovers the Ruling Cause, the Universal Scheme as he had the Divine Origin, the Creative Principle, the Universal Source and the Universal Soul in the

[1] 'Thoughts at Victoria Beach', *Africa Sings*, op. cit.
[2] Ibid.

earlier poem 'Awareness'. These are big words and still bigger concepts. Together with the free use of capitals, an adjective to every noun and a regular resort to the devices of pathetic fallacy and elision, they represent the popular pastiche of an age when bombast was the best weapon in the armoury of the freedom fighter.

Bombast served on the one hand to prove Young Africa had become the equal, if not the better, of the Englishman at his own language, and on the other it served to confuse and befuddle the adulating mob. The woolly-thinking nationalist had only to fire off a string of -isms unknown to the masses and they went delirious with thunderous cheers for a hero who was a walking book. By the time of Mr Okara's entry into the field of poetry such gimmicks had quite exhausted themselves. Recluse or aristocrat, the poet no longer was of the people. Withdrawn into himself, his problems had become his own, his language one constantly geared to express issues personal to his own sensibility. The day of short circuit for both poet and public had set in.

With the later poets, the new dimension of achievement is perhaps not always realized sufficiently for the picture to be instantly visible to a large section of an already limited audience. My own 'The Imprisonment of Obatala' provides a notorious example about which pupils and teachers alike are constantly writing in to the poet for exposition! And I dare say Mr Soyinka's new long poem 'Idanre' will be regarded by many as carrying a similar if not stronger dose of constipation. Difficult though 'The Imprisonment of Obatala' may be, it can be said without presumption that the poem demands no more of the reader than does Mr W. H. Auden's poem 'Music des Beaux Arts'. Just as a knowledge of Greek mythology and of the painting by Brueghel is essential for anything like a full appreciation of the Auden poem, so is a knowledge of Yoruba mythology and of the painting by Susanne Wenger a considerable aid to an understanding of 'The Imprisonment of Obatala'. But obviously both Yoruba culture and Nigerian poet labour under a handicap beside Greek civilization and

73

the maestro Auden. Add to this those two old disabilities first diagnosed by Dr I. A. Richards a quarter of a century ago and very rampant today among readers of poetry in Nigeria, by which I mean inhibition and a proneness to stock response, and the chances of the poet making the touchline are lame indeed.

To switch metaphors, it must be admitted that a culture curtain or culture gap does exist between poet and public, sometimes only partially so, particularly where the poet draws upon one individual subject or incident that can be programmed by way of brief notes, as in Mr Soyinka's 'Abiku' and mine; at other times as in Mr Soyinka's 'Idanre' where a poet is consciously exploiting a whole system of thought that is of occult nature, then the curtain or gap between the uninitiated public and the poet can be complete and prohibitive.

The average teacher of poetry in Nigeria, trained only in the appreciation of traditional English poetry, exhibits very strongly built-in reactions against modern Nigerian poetry, indeed against all modern poetry, and therefore cannot easily accommodate novelty. Possessed of reflexes conditioned as those of Pavlov's dog, he reacts readily to any item out of the double vistas of the Classics and the Bible that according to Grierson inform English poetry. But the slightest reference to the religion, history and oral traditions of his own peoples leaves him sniffing at once for explanations. With an audience of such listeners the break with the artist may be considered as complete. It is however not irreparable. For the public it is a matter of overcoming its own psychological and educational inertia; for the poet one for coming out of his often cryptic soul.

By way of postscript, we may add that modern Nigerian poetry provides a paradigm for modern African poetry. That is, the phenomenon of communication we have tried to establish here for one country also obtains for a good area of the continent—that south of the Sahara. Projecting this line of communication between poet and public, we find that M Léopold Sedar Senghor and others of his Negritude School as well as the Ghanaian Mr Kwesi Dei Anang and Mr Frank Kobina Parkes have their place by the Nigerian pioneer nationalist poet Chief Dennis Osadebay; the Ghanaian poet Mr George Awoonor-Williams and the Congolese Mr Felix Utamsi Tchikaya have positions among the Nigerians, Mr Gabriel Okara, Mr Wole Soyinka, Mr Christopher Okigbo and myself, while the South African poet Mr Dennis Brutus falls a little beyond them in catching the ear of a growing international audience that professes great concern for Apartheid and yet does very little towards eradicating this obnoxious system. Mr Kofi Awoonor, we may add, stands nearer Mr Okara, while Mr Utamsi Tchikaya, and incidentally the two Malagasyan poets M. Jean-Joseph Rabearivele and M. Jacques Rabemananjara can fairly be placed beside Mr Okigbo in this line of communication.

It will be noted that a number of poets have not been included in our classification. The reason is simple. These poets, though featuring regularly in anthologies, have not as yet been published in full length or as individuals. This is a criterion first raised by the South African author Mr Ezekiel Mphahlele in rebuke of us at the Berlin Conference of Poets in 1964 for listing him and a number of others as South African poets. It seems to me one well worth observing all the time by those whose business it is to set up poets, playwrights and novelists in Africa. But even this variety of poets appearing only in anthologies and periodicals will be seen on closer examination to fit somewhere into our theory of the communication line existing between poet and public in contemporary Africa.

4: *Aspects of Nigerian drama*

If drama means the elegant imitation of some action significant to a people, if this means the physical representation or
the evocation of one poetic image or a complex of such
images, if the vital elements to such representation or evocation are speech, music, ritual, song as well as dance and mime,
and if as the Japanese say of their Noh theatre, the aim is to
open the ear of the mind of a spectator in a corporate
audience and open his eyes to the beauty of form, then there
is drama in plenty in Nigeria, much of this as distinctive as any
in China, Japan and Europe. But drama of what beginning,
of how many kinds, of what form, and in what language? Are
its functions solely aesthetic and of entertainment value as in
Europe and America, or have these functions, in addition,
ceremonial and spiritual relevance for both actors and spectators? To shed a measure of light upon a subject so much in the
news these days and yet so much misunderstood by so many,
satisfactory answers must be found to these queries, and I
dare say, several besides.

Of the origins of Nigerian drama very little is known that is
reliable and precise, for the simple reason that no comprehensive study has been made so far of the subject either by the
old government sociologists or by the new drama exponents
of today. But one fact is certain. Contrary to what some seem
to think, Nigerian drama did not begin at the University of
Ibadan. The roots go beyond there, and one hopes they are
more enduring than that. Very likely, they lie where they have
been found among other peoples of the earth, deep in the past
of the race. Writes Sir James Fraser in *The Golden Bough*:

> . . . according to a widespread belief, which is not with a foundation

in fact, plants reproduce their kinds through the sexual union of male and female elements, and that on the principle of homoeopathic or imitative magic, this reproduction is supposed to be stimulated by the real or mock marriage of men and women who masquerade for the time being as spirits of vegetation. Such magical dramas have played a great part in the popular festivals of Europe, and based as they are on a very wide conception of natural law, it is clear that they must have been handed down from a remote antiquity.[1]

We are told later this magical theory of the seasons became supplemented by a religious theory:

For although men now attributed the annual cycle of change primarily to corresponding changes in their deities, they still thought that by performing certain magical rites they could aid the god, who was the principle of life, in his struggle with the opposing principle of death . . . *There ceremonies which they observed for this purpose were in substance a dramatic representation of the natural processes which they wished to facilitate* [italics are mine]; for it is a familiar tenet of magic that you can produce any desired effect by merely imitating it. And as they now explained the fluctuations of growth and decay, of reproduction and dissolution, by the marriage, the death, and the rebirth of revival of the gods, the irreligious or rather magical dramas turned in great measure on these themes.[2]

We have drawn extensively upon the well-worn handbook because we believe that, as the roots of European drama go back to the Egyptian Osiris and the Greek Dionysius, so are the origins of Nigerian drama likely to be found in the early religious and magical ceremonies and festivals of the peoples of this country. The *egungun* and *oro* of the Yoruba, the *egwugwu* and masques of the Ibo, and the *owu* and *oru* water masquerades of the Ijaw are dramas typical of the Nigerian national repertory still generally unacknowledged today.

Now Nigerian drama falls into two broad groups. One we may call traditional, the other modern drama. Of the first, still very much in the original state described by Frazer, we can again determine two main sub-groups. One of these is sacred because its subjects and aims are religious, while the

---

[1] *The Golden Bough* (London, Macmillan).
[2] Ibid.

other is secular drama shading from the magical through a number of sub-kinds to the straight play and entertainment piece. Within the sacred species there are again two types: one grouping together what have been variously termed ancestral or myth plays, and the other which are masquerades or plays, by age groups and cults. The dramas of Obatala and Oshagiyan performed annually at Oshogbo and Ejigbo provide indisputable examples of the first sacred kind. Against this set are the masquerades, for example, the *ekine* plays of Buguma.

Covering the Oshagiyan festival at Ejigbo, M. Pierre Verger, the French ethnologist shunting between Brazil and here, reports that a 'miniature war' opens the festival with a real bang. This is fought between the twin wards of Isale Osholo and Oke Mapo. 'Composed of attacks, hasty withdrawals and offensive sallies', the battle 'is interspersed with periods of comparative calm, during which the combatants' standing up their special fighting sticks 'no longer attack their enemies but shout invectives and insults at each other worthy of the age of Homer'. In earlier times, the fighting was simply symbolic, being staged between the priests. But the epic staging today calls up all able-bodied men of the clan so that they can taste of the injuries their ancestors administered to the Rain-maker who denied them rain. It is this version that M. Pierre Verger found still observed in Bahia today.

The annual ritual imprisonment of Obatala is not unlike that of the crucified Christ. Obatala in fact is the creation God of the Yoruba. Though all-powerful, he is gentle and full of love for all creation. In the legend, against the advice of the Oracle Ifa, Obatala, on his way to Sango, the God of Thunder, relieves Eshu, the God of Mischief, here disguised as an old woman, of a pot of oil. The pot breaks in the process with an effect like a sacred vessel breaking—which is not unlike that of opening Pandora's box! Thus Obatala, his white dress all dripping with oil, arrives at the court of King Sango at Oyo, and since nobody recognizes the God, he is thrown into jail when he protests at the ill-treatment of a horse. As a result, drought and famine befall the earth. And it is not until King Sango consults the oracle and is told he must make reparation to an innocent man wrongly punished in his kingdom that the general curse is lifted. This is the story re-enacted in the annual ritual at Oshogbo and other Yoruba towns, a story which has informed my own problematic poem 'The Imprisonment of Obatala'.

In each case given above, the story derives directly from an ancestor or founder myth well known to the audience, and the development is not so much by logic and discussion as by a poetic evocation of some religious experience shared alike by performer and spectators as in ancient Greece. For them the act is therefore one of worship and sacrifice.

A similar drama is described with tremendous power by Mr Chinua Achebe in *The Arrow of God*. This is The First Coming of Ullu, as celebrated in the market-place of 'the six villages of Umuaro' to the clamorous beat of the ikolo and ogene. The precipitate entrance of the protagonist priest Ezeulu, all got up in his regalia and waving his Nne Ofo ahead of his assistants, the pantomime he breaks into, the monologue and incantation he says while the participating audience waves leaves of pumpkin in offering of prayer, the dumping of these into a heap in burial of the sins of the land to the crescendo and crash of the kome, and the sudden stampede of the six settlements of Umuaro out of the square now inherited by spirits—this is highly stylized drama indeed. One can only hope that the great havoc and tornado that was Winterbota, I mean, Captain Winterbottom, Her Britannic Majesty's Political Agent accredited to one of the primitive tribes of the Lower Niger in their own interest and for their pacification, did not irrecoverably blow down this splendid institution of Ullu of the Six Settlements.

In all this the elements of pleasure and entertainment cannot be neatly pared from the devotion and ecstasy of religious worship. In the masquerade and age plays the aesthetic experience of the art undoubtedly is dominant. In fact the anthropologist Mr Robin Horton more or less states they are

79

purely so. This is what he says in *Africa*, of the New Year
Festival of Buguma:

> The ekine plays are overtly religious in purpose, and those of the
> young men more or less unashamedly secular; both traditional and
> modern performances contain a very large element of sheer recrea-
> tion. As art, all these masquerades are best judged as ballet rather
> than drama: though there is a plot of sorts running through many
> of them, it is at best very slight—rather a framework upon which
> to hang a dance sequence than something of value in itself. The leg
> of the dancer, not the story he enacts, is what Kalabari praise and
> criticize.[1]

Mr Horton makes the same point in respect of the Amagba
Festival at another Ijaw settlement, that of Kula, a point with
which we are not wholly in agreement and hope to take up
later.

It is in a similar vein the novelist Mr Onuora Nzekwu
reports in *Nigeria Magazine* on the production of the *Mingi
Oporopo*, that is, the water-pig, at Opobo:

> The drama . . . reveals a high standard of play-acting . . . the various
> parts fit the daily life of the actors and tend to make the whole
> performance more real and natural.
>
> The play was enacted not in the river, but in the Amayanabo's
> compound. Of course, there was a canoe, paddles, a fishing net,
> representation of the shrines to the god of fortune. Fish and the
> monster were represented by masquerades whose carved headpieces
> told the role each played. The headpiece, a large fish, depicting the
> monster and which can open and shut its mouth at will is a credit
> to the creative ability of those people.[2]

On the secular plane the stage is equally crowded. First,
there are the 'magic' or trick plays and secondly the pastoral
or puppet plays like those of Calabar described with such
mixed feeling by that proconsul and anthropologist P. A.
Talbot. Incidentally, his works are quite a jungle—as thick as
any he wandered through in southern Nigeria at the first
quarter of the century. The interesting thing is that they carry

[1] *Africa*, xxxiii, No. 2, April 1963.
[2] *Nigeria Magazine*, No. 63, 1969.

in their labyrinthine way pathways that often lead to un-
expected clearings and discoveries. One such surprise is his
record of a number of plays performed for him during his
tours among the Efik and Ibibio people. One was *The Tight-
rope Dancer* or *The Second-born Excels*; another was *The Polo
Play*.

Talbot records in *Life in Southern Nigeria* that he thought
some of these mere 'conjuring tricks'; others he found to be
'gruesome plays', especially those in which either a baby was
professedly pounded to death in a mortar and then brought to
life again whole, or the decapitated head of a man was slapped
back on his neck without apparent harm, or a man was im-
paled upon a spit without causing disgorgement of his bowels.
Another was staged by ventriloquists. According to Talbot,
this carried an incest interlude too 'vulgar' for entry into
official files.

> I am happy to say that this is the only occasion on which we have
> encountered an instance of real vulgarity among primitive African
> peoples. Up till now, even when turning on subjects usually avoided
> by Europeans on account of difficulty of treatment, the perfect
> simplicity of manner and purpose with which such were mentioned
> or explained robbed them of possible offence. In this one case,
> most unfortunately inexcusable and irrelevant coarseness showed
> itself, naked and unashamed, and we could not but wonder as to the
> influence to which the innovation was due.[1]

What was this innovation that riled the old resident so? We
gather it was open copulation between father and daughter-
in-law. Obviously at that point of the performance, life had
overcome art!

But the day was not completely lost; in fact it had a
splendid finale, one well worth the dangers of the expedition
taken in a hammock:

> After the garishness and coarseness of the performance above
> described, we were quite unprepared for the beauty of that which
> was to follow.[2]

[1] *Life in Southern Nigeria* (London, Frank Cass, pp. 72–86).
[2] Ibid.

This was the Akan play *Utughu* or *The Spider Play*. Preparations for it were always intense for 'as in everything Africa, Tragedy walked close upon the heels of Comedy'. Obviously very moved, Talbot goes on to describe the Female Figure in the special costume she wore at the point she does a death duet with her partner in this 'puppet' play:

> She wore a mask, brightest gold in colour, which, from the distance, looked as though it might have come straight from some Egyptian tomb. Here were the same long diamond-shaped eyes as those which gaze from old papyri or the walls of many a forgotten sepulchre, newly opened to the light of day, or such as are depicted on painted sarcophagi or the papyri of *The Book of Dead*.[1]

After the performance, Talbot's wish to have his wife photograph 'the loveliness of the gold-painted mask worn by the bird-wife' was granted by the Ibibio 'on the payment of the requested dash'. But then comes the shock:

> Our disillusionment may be imagined when the actual objects were laid in our hands. Carved from a solid block of wood, almost grotesque in outline, the whole glamour and beauty of the thing seemed to have disappeared by magic . . . Thinking over the difference, scarce believable save to those who had actually witnessed it, a memory wave brought to mind visions of masks worn in the dramas of old Greece. There, too, the conditions were not unlike. Given here, in the open—possibly also with a background of swaying palms—may not the glamour of air and sky have lent to these masks also, when seen from a distance, a beauty and aloofness which not only heightened the effect of the glorious text, but gave to the whole an atmosphere in which great men and women lived and acted greatly—far removed from the commonplaces of this work-a-day world?[2]

The point to remember in this gorgeous piece of rhetoric is that about the thin line existing between reality and illusion in the theatre. If, as both Dr Johnson and Coleridge enjoin us, we never quite lose all our consciousness while willingly suspending our sense of disbelief, there will be no cause to rush the stage at the point when Hamlet is hacking Laertes to death. This is a custom and convention strictly observed in

[1] *Life in Southern Nigeria* (London, Frank Cass, pp. 72–86).
[2] Ibid.

many of our societies, else what prevents the housewife or child from telling the man from the mask? It will be good too to recognize a point about such comparisons. The implication is not that one group of people borrowed this and that property from another but that there can and in fact there do occur areas of coincidence and correspondence in the way of living among several peoples separated by vast distances and time, and who apparently are of distinct cultures, practices and persuasions. For example, the orchestra and the leader-chorus arrangement of characters occupies as much a principal part in Nigerian theatre as it did in Greek theatre. But this is not to say one is debtor to the other. It is a matter of correspondence and coincidence. Yeats observed this to be true, seeing in every Irish beauty a potential Helen full of havoc to the race. And the husband and wife team of Herskovits underline the fact with obvious excitement when in Dahomey they discovered in *The Lover and the Initiate*, a cult drama, the old Greek story of Alcestis:

> '(here) the conventional unities are observed. The place is the cult-house; the action occurs during one day; the theme is love and the courage to defy the *Vodum* and Death in its name, until both are moved to pity.'

This leads us directly into our third class of secular drama—the civic kind. Mainly drawn from myths and rituals telling the history of the tribe, they serve a common civic purpose as do tales and fables, namely, that of educating and initiating the young into the secrets and moral code of society. It is interesting to note that both the period of eight years, during which time the Dahomean initiate was interned in the forest away from female contact, and the purpose of turning him into a responsible citizen are themes that feature in the graduation drama of *Isiji* or *Ipu Ogo* performed by the Ibo people of Edda near Afikpo in eastern Nigeria.

Another beautiful drama of the same class, associated with a figure of antiquity and now observed more or less as a vegetation festival is the annual *Igogo* at Owo in western Nigeria. The central figure is Orosen, wife of the founder of Owo. A changeling creature from the forest, the story of how her rival spouses eventually encompass her downfall by tricking their man into revealing the true identity of his favourite wife throws vivid light upon the conventional day to day conflicts and complexities obtaining in every house of polygamy.

Our fourth class of the secular kind consists of dance or song dramas such as the Udje of the Urhobo. The Udje

> is straight entertainment. That is, it is all art and little or no ritual and religion. Performance is by age groups, wards and towns, each using the other as subject for its songs.

More often than not, the songs are straight satirical pieces, although a good number are parables passing oblique social comments and criticism. Supplemented with imitative action and movement, however much on a linear level, these song and dance dramas never fail to reach their audience, members of whom break out from time to time to join in the act with the cast. Quite similar to these are the seasonal dance-dramas of the Ijaw, Ekpetese being easily the best known of the lot. But that was thirty odd years ago, and besides, its stars and fans are all either faded or scattered.

Finally, the narrative or epic dramas which go on for days (seven is the magic number!) and which, because they demand so much energy and time, are more or less dying out today. A ready example is the Ijaw saga of *Ozidi*. Out of this half drama, half narrative work I have made a marathon play of the same name while work is at present in progress to publish the original story both in the Ijaw and English. It is the story of a posthumous son brought up by a witch grandmother to avenge an equally famous father killed at war by his own compatriots to spite their idiot king his brother. But the hero overreaches himself in the course of his quest for vengeance, and in a grand turn of dramatic irony narrowly misses his doom at the hands of Smallpox. In its roll-call of characters, range of action, and tone of poetry and colour, this is classic drama which we have shot on film and which we hope will show beyond the shores of Ijaw.

So much for the various kinds of traditional drama. Now how many are there of the type we have called modern? Two, if our count is correct. One is the folk theatre of Hubert Ogunde, Kola Ogunmola, Duro Ladipo and their several imitators, and the second is what some have called literary drama. Some would say the latter has its heart right at home here in Nigeria and its head deep in the wings of American and European theatre! The works of Mr Wole Soyinka, Dr Ene Henshaw, and my own plays, I am told, clearly bear this badge, but whether of merit or infamy it is a matter still in some obscurity. Of the former kind, however, Chief Ulli Beier, writing for *Nigeria Magazine* under the assumed name of 'Critic', was pleased to echo British opinions that *Oba Koso* by Duro Ladipo is representative of 'a new art form ... neither opera, nor ballet nor poetic drama but all the three perfectly fused together'.[1]

The emphasis in the above statement really ought to be on the fusion process, for the fact is that music, dance, and poetry have been the constants of true Nigerian drama from the earliest birth-marriage-and-death-cycle ceremonies and rituals to our own current exercises and experiments. The traditional theatre of sacred and secular dramas we have tried to outline here, from the ancestral to the epic plays, really is this 'closely unified combination of the arts' lost to Europe and America a long time ago. The difference has been in the variation, that is, the degree of the mixture these vital elements to drama undergo from play to play, place to place, each according to the purpose motivating the act. Thus for most, the ascendant elements are those of music, dance, ritual and mime, that of speech being subdued to a minimum. This minimal use of dialogue is probably due to the fact that a good number of these plays belong to some particular group or cult in society and therefore require a certain atmosphere and

[1] *Nigeria Magazine*, No. 87, Dec. 1965.

amount of secrecy and awe. Silence can be an active agent of this. And because there is often little speech between characters outside of the invocations and incantations, it is easy to dismiss many traditional pieces either as simple pageants and processions or at best as forms close to opera and ballet.

The achievement then of the folk theatre of the Ogunmola and Ladipo kind is that it has found the happy means between these ancient constants and the much newer ones of overall speech and plot or lack of it demanded by modern theatre. They have invented no new form. The English translation of Duro Ladipo's plays by Chief Ulli Beier in fact shows these to be no more than simple poetic dramas dependent on the accumulated image and utterance realized on a linear progression. These are no different from others of their species. But in the Yoruba, when not stripped of their concomitant music, dance and ritual, the total effect is terrific and different, and for a white man who has seen nothing like that since Boadicea and the Valkyrie, the impact is that of a clean knock-out.

Very likely, the so-called literary theatre of Nigeria is beginning to miss this complete identity of purpose and response enjoyed increasingly by the folk theatre in Yoruba. Its latest plays show a definite tendency towards this composite art of the folk theatre. *Kongi's Harvest* by Mr Wole Soyinka, Mr Frank Aig-Imoukhuede's *Ikeke*, and my own *Ozidi* provide concrete evidence for this view. Whether this is a deliberate adoption of a principle, and whether working in English as these playwrights do, they will succeed in wedding that medium to Nigerian drum, song and dance is another matter and one for their individual talents.

An aspect of Nigerian drama acclaimed by even those who do not as yet acknowledge the existence of this art so expressive of our culture is the wealth and variety of its masks, costumes and make-up. Talbot at the turn of the century went lyrical over the fact. Today the apparatus, a super-admixture of the symbolic and the naturalistic, still inspires instant applause and awe in the Nigerian theatre, indigenous or imported. As against this is the minimum use of sets and props outside the ritual paraphernalia, a fact that is also well known for giving imagination full play.

But two aspects not so well noted by many are the use of interpolated exclamation in Nigerian drama and the regular phenomenon of 'possession'. One is the spontaneous, independent outburst of cheering, directed to group or self, by members of the audience and players themselves. Together with music and dance as well as common story, which are obvious properties shared by all, this provides the spectator with that direct means of participation in the production so remarkable in Nigerian drama.

The other is the incidence of 'possession'. This is the attainment by actors in the heat of performance of 'actual freedom of spirit from this material world', a state of transformation which has been given the rather sniggering name of 'possession' or 'auto-intoxication' by those outside its sphere of influence and sympathy. This phenomenon features regularly in sacred plays, especially the masquerade kind. It was a constant cause of hold-ups in my filming of the Ozidi saga at Oruȧ. And such is the fear of the possible danger an actor may cause himself and others, when in this state of complete indentification with his role, that leading irate masquerades in Ibo and Ijaw are usually provided with leashes held back or paid out accordingly by attendants. Nor could this state be a totally passive one, for at that point when as the Ijaw put it, 'things unseen enter the man', the actor may become a medium, a votary of some ancestor spirits or divine powers filling him with the gift of prophecy.

Quite tied up with this phenomenon is the observance of certain taboos in a number of plays within the Nigerian repertory. Thus priests and worshippers of Obatala must not eat certain meals, nor wear any dress other than white. Performance of sacred dramas like that of Oshagiyan at Ejigbo cannot just be fixed for any day of the week. It must fall within only those that are holy to the deity. In the epic drama of Ozidi, the story-teller/protagonist may not have anything to do with women in the course of the seven-day production! This seems to be a carry-over of habits from the character to the player, a practice perhaps also applicable to other parts and other plays subject to particular taboos.

Now what are all these in aid of? Why the precarious preparations so fascinating to old Talbot? Why the risk of observing taboos the breaking of which spells punishment and possible death? In the conventional Western theatre, life, though hazardous, is led for pure commerce and entertainment. Nigerian theatre, that is, its modern department, seems to incline that way. But traditional Nigerian theatre, so very much part of the contour of life in this country, what functions does it fulfil? Let us return to Mr Robin Horton with whom we said we had a little bone to pick:

> The masquerade belies the easy and oft-heard generalization that in traditional West African culture there was no such thing as Art for Art's sake. For although its performance is intimately associated with religious activity and belief, here it is the religion that serves the art, rather than vice versa. It is possible that some studies of West African culture have not found art practised for its own sake, simply because they have not looked for it in the right direction. This brings us to the second point. In describing the masquerade performance, I took pains to stress that its central element was the dance, and that the apparatus of costume and headpiece filled a subordinate place in the whole. I also stressed that the sculpted mask was first and foremost an instrument for securing the presence of a spirit, and not something produced as a work of art. This in fact is true of Kalabari sculpture generally. Now it would be dangerous to generalize on the basis of this one example. But taken together with reports on some other West African cultures such as that of the Ibo, it does make one suspect, at least in certain areas of West Africa, the dance overshadows sculpture, painting, architecture and literature as the leading traditional art.[1]

Mr Horton's area of reference is rather wide. But it is true as he says that there is pure art in these parts. Limiting ourselves to a more compact area as we have tried to do, we can

[1] Loc. cit.

point straight at our popular Agbor dancers and several seasonal dances of the kind staged by the young everywhere in this country. Mr Horton, however, is unfortunate in his choice of illustration. The Ijaw masquerade, that of Kalabari included, has always served a religious purpose quite apart from its entertainment value. In every Ijaw settlement there is a corpus of masquerade for every age-group of men. This ranges from toddlers in an ascending order to grizzle-headed elders, the degree of religiousness being in direct proportion to the position each occupies in the age hierarchy. The virgin palm fronds girding the headpiece of the chief masquerade, the fences of similar fronds this masquerade cuts through in his initial passage into town, the actual sacrifice of gin and cockerel the priest makes to it on the field of play, these certainly are conscious acts of worship without which there can be neither performance for pleasure nor peace for the age-group. What is more, the chief masquerade of the eldest group to which all adult males eventually graduate provides in many places the centre for a prominent communal shrine. The Oguberi at Kiagbodo and the masquerade of Kikoru at Okrika are such gods sporting powerful priests and to whom members of the community are asked by oracles in times of trouble to send prayers and individual offerings. Mr Horton is therefore somewhat playing it down when he gives the Ijaw masquerade as an example of art practised for art's sake in West Africa.

Indeed, it is doubtful whether any of the examples we have given of traditional Nigerian drama serve purely aesthetic ends. First, as Mr Horton himself admits, the very myths upon which many of these dramas are based, so beautiful in themselves, serve to record the origins and *raison d'être* of the institutions and peoples who own them. Secondly, dramas, like the Ijaw masquerade and Ullu ritual, represent spirits and gods which their worshippers seek to propitiate in the manner described by Frazer. They are therefore manifestations of a special religion. Thirdly, they serve a civic and social purpose by educating and initiating the young into the ways and duties of the community. In the process they help to knit together persons of similar background, giving them a common identity. Fourthly, as stated by the historian Dr E. J. Alagoa,[1] masquerade dramas foster good relations between members of one village and another. A people famous for their performance will always have spectators pouring in from everywhere to see their show. In other words, the masquerade can in fact become a town's best advertisement. Fifthly, these dramas, whether sacred or otherwise, often provide the one occasion in the year that brings home all true native sons and daughters resident and scattered abroad. This is the occasion for thanksgiving, allowing celebrants the double opportunity to report home and show off whatever priceless possessions they have won from their labours abroad. Sixthly, some induce that state of mind when the spirit is temporarily freed of its flesh shackles and the medium is invested with extra tongues that can foretell any imminent disaster, and if possible, prescribe prevention. A seventh use that Nigerian drama is put to is to be found in the Urhobo drama-dance Udje which is a vehicle for social comment, satire and sheer spread of meaty gossip. And last but equally vital, like all good drama, the Nigerian one is robust entertainment.

One aspect of this drama is still left to examine, that of language. It is a mixed blessing that no text exists of many of the several examples we have given of Nigerian theatre. Mixed blessing because it saves us on the one hand the trouble of proving any special point, while on the other, it underlines the sad fact that there are such mines of material lying around to be dug up for our national enrichment. But it can safely be said that each traditional piece, in the way that T. S. Eliot outlined for poetry in the theatre, does pride to the language of its people at all levels of meanings. So we believe does the folk theatre at present mainly in Yoruba.

The difficulty and controversy come when we move into the department of modern drama in Nigeria—drama that is

___
[1] 'Delta Masquerades' in *Nigeria Magazine*, No. 97, June 1967.

usually seen in print before it is seen on the stage. The dispute has to do with that irascible hobby-horse of scholars like my friend Mr Obiajunwa Wali who foresees a dead end to African literature written in European languages. But I would not like now to be taken on that John Gilpin ride! Can it be valid and authentic literature? asks Mr A. Bodurin in the *African Statesman*. He goes on with the voice of dogma:

> In literature content and expression determine each other so funda-mentally that the validity and authenticity of a work suffers as soon as the native content is expressed in a foreign language. This dissociation of content from expression is partly responsible for the difficulty in appreciating Wole Soyinka's plays. I am strongly convinced that if *A Dance of the Forests*, the most intriguing of his plays, were written in Yoruba, much of the obscurity would dis-appear.[1]

Now let me quote another piece of castigation, this time of me.

> The usual criticism of Mr Clark's plays is that he has not quite found the kind of verse suitable for the presentation of dramatic action. This is, in my view, a just criticism. It is probably not con-soling to add that Shakespeare did not begin to write good dramatic poetry till 1599, that is, till his tenth year in the theatre. No one ever begins by tossing off masterpieces. The delineation of character which is one of the springs of dramatic poetry is naturally a late accomplishment. One has to be much more than a gifted lyricist even to create ordinary dialogue that is resourceful, natural, and imaginative while dealing with the drab details which are bound to find their way into a play.[2]

That is Mr Ben Obumselu reviewing my play *The Raft* (or was it Mr Soyinka's production of it?) in *Ibadan*. After citing a passage which he never stops to analyse, he romps home:

> Mr Clark has not, as a dramatist, been fortunate in the kind of poetry he has admired. The . . . actors found it difficult to decide whether they were uneducated Nigerian lumbermen who spoke English indifferently, or poetic personages to whom imaginative poetry came naturally. Occasionally, they strayed into pidgin English rhythms as lumbermen. I doubt whether Mr Clark con-sidered this matter sufficiently.

[1] *African Statesman*, i, No. 1, 1965.
[2] *Ibadan*, No. 19, June 1964.

I would like to assure Mr Obumselu that I considered the matter most sufficiently. The characters in *The Raft* and in other plays of mine are neither 'poetic personage' nor the kind of Cockney he has in mind. They are ordinary Ijaw persons working out their life's tenure at particular points on the stage. And they are speaking in their own voices and language to an audience members of whom they expect to reach with a reasonable degree of sympathy and conviction. At this point, I would like to quote a letter I wrote from America in 1963 on this very subject to Mr Gerald Moore, who on first reading the manuscript of my play *The Masquerade*, objected to the words *privy*, *phenomenon* and *truncated* on the lips of Ijaw villagers:

> Education and class-consciousness which pre-suppose and actually create levels of speech and language in European societies have, thank God, not done that havoc to the non-literate tongues like Ijaw. Style, imagery, etc., these are what tell one user of a language from another—not grammar or class; for we haven't that. And you very well know that all I consider myself is a letter-writer for my characters.

In other words, the task for the Ijaw and, I dare say, any Nigerian or African artist, writing in a European language like English, is one of finding the verbal equivalent for his characters created in their original and native context. The quest is not on the horizontal zone of dialect and stress which are classifications of geography, society, and education. It is on the vertical plane of what the schoolmasters call style and register, that is, a matter of rhetoric, the artistic use and conscious exploitation of language for purposes of persuasion and pleasure. If in the process, there occurs no 'dissociation of content and expression' as Mr Bodurin puts it, and I understand that term to mean, say, the discussion of food prices by market-women in the jargon of biologists, but on the contrary, there is a faithful reproduction of the speech habits of one people into another language as Mr Chinua Achebe does significantly in English with the Ibo dialogue proceeding by technique of the proverb, then I think the artist has achieved a reasonable measure of success.

In this connection, I would like to draw attention to the use of another language device, that of indirection which features prominently in my own play *Song of a Goat*. That doctor and patient in that play do not approach the business on hand with the directness of an arrow does not mean the playwright is unappreciative of the importance of speed and despatch. Rather, it is a recognition by him of a living convention observed among the people of the community treated in the play, namely, that you do not rush in where angels fear to tread for the simple reason that the flying arrow either kills promptly or sends the bird in flight. Accordingly, delicate issues are handled delicately by these people. This approach is evident in their manner of negotiating marriage between one family and another, and of announcing the news of death to the persons most affected. Each subject is tackled by indirection.

This is not to say the Nigerian playwright and novelist writing in English will not sometimes use the old gradation of speech as understood by all of us from our reading of European literature. Indeed some do use pidgin, like Mr Wole Soyinka in his play *Brother Jero*, Mr Cyprian Ekwensi in his novel *Jagua Nana*, and Mr Chinua Achebe in his latest terrifyingly prophetic and exact story *A Man of the People*. But the character using pidgin must be in a position to do so in actual life, and there must be a special purpose served. That is, there must be propriety. Thus the houseboy will speak to his master in our new urban social set-up in the pidgin that his education and class dictate. Similarly the Warri market-woman selling to a cosmopolitan clientele will use the pidgin that really is the *lingua franca* of that section of the country.

In Mr Wole Soyinka's *Brother Jero*, however, the disciple Chume oscillates between pidgin and the so-called standard or Queen's English. The excuse might be that at one time the situation demands that he speaks straight in English, that is, pidgin English as befits an office messenger, while at another it requires him to speak in his original Nigerian tongue here translated into appropriate standard English as we have said.

But is this really so? Chume enters speaking standard English with his wife:

> *Chume*: Is there anything else before I go?
> *Amope*: You've forgotten the mat. I know it's not much but I would like something to sleep on . . .
> *Chume*: You've got a bed at home.
> *Amope*: And so I'm to leave my work undone. My trade is to suffer because I have a bed at home . . .
> *Chume*: I am nearly late for work.[1]

It could be conceded that husband and wife here are speaking in their original tongue and that the playwright has simply rendered this into the equivalent English. The wife in fact maintains this level of language all through the play. In other words, she sticks to her tongue, a sharp one, all the time.

Not so the husband. After that slanging-match, we find him soliciting the prophet's help:

> *Chume*: Brother Jero, you must let me beat her!
> *Jero*: What!
> *Chume*: (desperately): Just once, Prophet. Just once.
> *Jero*: Brother Chume!
> *Chume*: Just once. Just one sound beating, and I swear not to ask again.
> *Jero*: Apostate. Have I not told you the will of God in this matter?
> *Chume*: But I have got to beat her, Prophet. You must save me from madness.
> *Jero*: I will. But only if you obey me.
> *Chume*: If anything else, Prophet. But for this one, make you let me just beat 'am once.
> *Jero*: Apostate!
> *Chume*: I n' go beat am too hard. Just once small small.
> *Jero*: Traitor!
> *Chume*: Just this once time. I no go ask again. Just do me this one favour, make a beat 'am today.[2]

This switch from standard to broken English by Chume may be an effective dramatic device for underscoring the reduction of personality in the disciple aimed at all the time by the Prophet, but read outside and away from the illusion of the

---

[1] *Brother Jero*, from *Three Short Plays* (London, O.U.P., 1969).
[2] Ibid.

theatre, it raises the problem of consistency not only in the matter of character but also in that of the playwright's art.

This seems to me a serious issue not resolved in the plays of Mr Wole Soyinka where pidgin English is employed. A signal monument of this is *The Road*. We need only sample the speech habits of the trainee-driver Salubi and Samson, the passenger-tout and driver's mate, to establish our case. Both begin in standard English, the vernacular equivalent:

> *Salubi*: Six o'clock I bet. I don't know how it is, but no matter when I go to sleep, I wake up when it strikes six. Now that is a miracle.
>
> (He gets out his chewing stick, begins to chew on it.)
>
> *Samson*: There is a miracle somewhere but not what you say. Maybe the sight of you using a chewing stick.
>
> *Salubi*: Look Samson, it's early in the morning.
>
> Go back to sleep if you're going to start that again.[1]

In the very next lines while Salubi tries on his chauffer's uniform, both characters change their level of speech, to a lower gear, so to speak:

> *Samson*: Who lend you uniform?
>
> *Salubi*: I buy it with my own money.

But only for the duration of those lines, for soon we return to the old gear:

> *Samson*: Second-hand.
>
> *Salubi*: So what?
>
> *Samson*: At least you might have washed it. Look at that bloodstain— has some one been smashing your teeth?

Then comes another abrupt change of levels, this time taken only by the driver-trainee:

> *Salubi*: Rubbish. Na palm-oil.
>
> *Samson*: All right, all right.
>
> But you are a funny person . . . How can anyone buy a uniform when he hasn't got a job?
>
> *Salubi*: Impression. I take uniform impress all future employer.

[1] *The Road* (London, O.U.P., 1965).

No doubt, very impressed himself, the passenger-tout and driver's mate suddenly shifts into the same number, however briefly:

> Samson: God Almighty. You dey like monkey
> wey stoway inside sailor suit.
> Salubi: Na common jealousy dey do you. I know I no get job, but I get uniform. (Starts to shine his brass buttons.)
> Samson (shakes his head): Instead of using all that labour to shine you buttons you should spare some for your teeth . . .

All this remains, for me at least, a baffling performance. Perhaps Mr Soyinka in his use of pidgin English is aiming at special theatric effects, too esoteric for common understanding, but it seems to me the playwright too would have done well to listen to his own Samson's advice, to wit, not to concentrate on one thing at the expense of another, especially when this is of equal if not greater importance. As it is, Mr Soyinka, in *The Road*, seems himself to have lost his way in the search for proper levels of speech for his odd collection of characters.

Well, there it is; but will our explanations satisfy the critics? One of them, I think Mr Bodurin, actually repeats the advice Mr Harold Hobson of the London *Sunday Times* was kind enough to give modern African playwrights free of charge, which was that they should forget they have been to universities. Perhaps the critics themselves should first take that advice. At the moment, many of them are encumbered with conventions and critical theories that pile up good grades in the old English schools, but then are thoroughly good for nothing thereafter. This is why, like the foreign 'rigorous teachers who seized their youths', these Nigerians require the special aid of programme notes setting out for them all strange practices as in Chinese and Japanese theatre. But then it is the lot of the artist often to be misunderstood.

5: Othello's useless scene

Othello has fifteen scenes—three in the first act, another three in the second, four in the third, a further three in the fourth, and finally, two scenes in the fifth act. Of these, the one opening the fourth act and running to line 211, that is, up to when 'a trumpet sounds' in Lodovico from Venice, is the scene with the flaw of repetition.

To have a place in the play, this scene ought in fact to begin with the stage direction: 'Enter Lodovico, Desdemona, and Attendants.' All that is new in the play follows upon this announcement, namely, the recall of Othello to Venice, his replacement by Cassio as the General Officer Commanding in Cyprus, and his striking of Desdemona:

> I am commanded home . . .
> Cassio shall have my place,

the general mumbles aloud as he reads the despatch.

These are the two items of news that for him prove the last straw. They feed his fury, being the actual worries now at work in his mind. Coming on top of Desdemona's ill-timed, importunate plea on behalf of the man he already suspects her with, they may very well account for why Othello strikes her:

> Is it his use?
> Or did the letters work upon his blood,
> And new-create this fault?

Lodovico's query underlines the point, the tragic change in the hero. And when Iago offers the information that 'He is much changed', we know for a fact that this had been accomplished long before in Scene 3 Act 3, that is, in the so-called corruption scene.

The real substance then of this other scene of corruption lies in the seventy-two lines at its end. The rest is superfluous to the plot of the play, neither advancing the action of it nor developing the character of any of the persons in it, least of all the hero. It is because the scenes in the first act all fulfil these functions in the story of the life and love of Othello that we all disagree with Dr Johnson that the play ought to have begun in the second act.

At this point, a definition of terms becomes necessary, and what better adjucator to call in our case against Shakespeare the master-tragedian than the very man who laid down the canon for tragedy? Said Aristotle: 'All plays alike possess spectacle, character, plot, diction, song, and thought. Of these elements the most important is the plot, *the ordering of the incidents.*' The italics are mine. Without disputing priorities with the old man, we would like to stress here that our subject is not the psychological study of character as of old nor of mood, situation, thought, whim or fantasy, as seems the case with the kitchen sink and *avant-garde* theatre today, *but* of plot as defined by Aristotle above, namely, '*the ordering of the incidents*' in a play. Elsewhere he calls this 'an ordered combination of incidents', and again, 'the arrangement of incidents'.

Such then is the plot. Aristotle goes on: '. . . the plot of a play, being the representation of an action, must present it as a unified whole; *and its various incidents must be so arranged that if any one of them is differently placed or taken away the effect of the wholeness will be seriously disrupted. For if the presence or absence of something makes no apparent difference, it is no real part of the whole.*' The italics again are mine. 'As for the stories', adds Aristotle, 'whether he is taking over something ready-made or inventing for himself the poet should first plan in general outline, and then expand by working out appropriate episodes.'

Our charge is that Shakespeare, in taking over 'the seventh novella of the third deca or decade of stories in the *Hecatommithi* by Giraldi Cinthio', broke the rules of plot, to the detriment of an otherwise great play. More than two-thirds of Scene 1 Act 4, as we have defined it and will endeavour to demonstrate, simply has no place in the plot of *Othello*.

Not only is this scene a repetition of action already presented; it is a travesty also of another principle set out by Aristotle for tragedy, that of 'reversal'. Now 'a reversal', he tells us, 'is a change from one state of affairs to its opposite, one which conforms . . . to probability or necessity'—like the temptation and fall of Othello in the true corruption scene which we shall soon examine.

'Reversal', Aristotle tells us, ought to accompany another device, that of 'discovery' which is the 'change from ignorance to knowledge, and it leads either to love or to hatred between persons destined for good or ill-fortune.' Together, these two provide 'the . . . most important means by which tragedy plays on our feelings, those of either pity or fear'. The tragedy of Othello is that, unlike Oedipus or his other avatars, he discovers nothing of fact. Oedipus, for example, in ignorance murdered his father, made love to his mother, had children that were his brothers and sisters, all of which provide him an irresistible lever to disaster. Othello on the other hand, acts merely upon malice and rumour peddled by one man. Hence the double pity of his 'reversal' of fortune. It carries no 'discovery' based on fact.

Reversal and discovery come to Othello in Scene 3 Act 3. Before then all we see of the man are those fine qualities of his: calm, confidence, and control as he meets the open threats of Brabantio and Roderigo at the Saggitary and court; his flight of imagination, wealth of experience, and quick mastery of military problems when he stands summoned before the Duke in council; his sense of discipline and duty as he answers the call to service even on the eve of a hard-won honeymoon; then finally in Cyprus, the uxurious husband side by side with the triumphant military governor of a turbulent island, meting emergency justice to his own immediate deputy. The emergent image of the man well deserves the part, that of 'a good man, who is not conspicuous for virtue and justice, and whose fall into misery is not due to vice and depravity, but rather to some error, a man who enjoys prosperity and a high reputation'.

Othello's one error of character, to use the words of the man all set to damn him, lies in the fact that:

> The Moor is of a free and open nature
> That thinks men honest that but seem to be so,
> And will as tenderly be led by the nose
> As asses are.

And lead tenderly by the nose as asses are is exactly what Iago does with Othello in Scene 3 Act 3. That the villain achieves so much in so short a time derives, we all accept, directly from a victim who proves so imaginative, so gullible, and so impressionable that he succumbs to every echo, every pause, every hint, and every platitude of Iago. 'Ha, I like not that.' 'No, sure, I cannot think it, / That he would steal away so guilty-like, / Seeing you coming.' 'Did Michael Cassio, / When you wooed my lady, know of your love?' 'Indeed!' 'Honest, my lord?' 'My lord, you know I love you.' 'Men should be what they seem; / Or those that be not, would they might seem none!' 'Utter my thoughts!' 'Who steals my purse steals trash—it is something, nothing / . . . But he that filches from me my good name / Robs me of that which not enriches him / And makes me poor indeed.' 'O, beware my lord, of jealousy. / It is the green-eyed monster!'

It takes exactly 182 lines to achieve the terrible change in Othello. 'Exchange me for a goat' he cries aloud in doubt in imagery already turning to the bestial. But he still retains some grip on his former self, still allows himself some small room for manoeuvre.

> I'll see before I doubt; when I doubt, prove;
> And on the proof, there is no more but this,
> Away at once with love or jealousy.

A man given to such fatalism, to making absolute choices like this would wait for just such a proof. But does Othello? Iago only has to say next—

> I know our country disposition well;
> In Venice they do let heaven see the pranks
> They dare not show their husbands, their best conscience
> Is not to leave it undone, but keep't unknown—

and that Desdemona 'did deceive her father, marrying' Othello, for the poor alien, ignorant of the ways of women in Venice and too willing to learn the worst, to declare in gratitude and self-damnation:

> I am bound to thee for ever.

After that, Iago can well indulge in under-statements and cheap tricks of auto-suggestion. 'I see this hath a little dashed your spirits' he commiserates with his master. 'Not a jot, not a jot' protests the general in greater agitation still. 'My lord, I see you're moved' Iago rubs it in, and when the Moor replies 'No, not much moved', his in fact has become a whine—so much so that the gallant man is unable to refute a single insult hurled at his wife by a common aide. All he can do is whine more: 'Why did I marry?'

From then on, after granting Iago immunity from prosecution and punishment for libel and defamation of his wife and himself, it is one headlong descent into the sewer of self-pity as regards his advanced age, his wild race, his poor education. By now, as we all know, he is a corrupted man speaking in images of corruption:

> I had rather be a toad,
> And live upon the vapour of a dungeon,
> Than keep a corner in the thing I love
> For others' uses. Yet 'tis the plague of great ones . . .

Desdemona's entry at this point serves as the signal for another of the man's romantic outbursts and proclamations of ideals:

> If she be false, O, then heaven mocks itself!
> I'll not believe't.

Believe what? one is inclined to ask.

Being so prone to auto-suggestion, the man proceeds directly to live and feel the part Iago has in a few lines created for him. 'I have a pain upon my forehead here' he declares himself a cuckold. Desdemona seeks to bind it with her handkerchief but 'he puts the handkerchief from him; and she drops it.' Thereupon Emilia picks it up to carry off to her husband. It should be noted that it is this same handkerchief that Othello bellows for in Act 3 Scene 4 that same day, believing that the loss of it is proof of his wife's infidelity. Either the horns grew straight out of his eyes so that he could not see fall what he put from him, or Desdemona herself was already too deranged to remember her napkin had dropped and that Emilia had been on hand to pick it up and return it to her.

Incidentally, a further query, that is usually explained with the theory of double-time, arises here. How could Iago, though the devil-incarnate that he is, have planned beforehand for Emilia to steal the handkerchief so that he could stage an act he was yet to hatch? Ready to hand is the convention of the soliloquy by which the audience is drawn in to play the confidante to the villian at every stage of his conspiracy against the hero. And Iago, we may add, almost always overexploits the device. Yet in this clear case of bungling on the part of the playwright all the honoured critics have been too ready to offer excuses and explanations. A. C. Bradley, in fact, in *Shakespearean Tragedy*, touches on it only by way of footnote:

> And neither she nor Othello observes what handkerchief it is. Else she would have remembered how she came to lose it, and would have told Othello; and Othello, too, would at once have detected Iago's lie (Act 3, Scene 3, line 438) that he had seen Cassio wipe his beard with the handkerchief 'to-day'. For in fact the handkerchief had been lost not an hour before Iago told that lie (line 288 of the same scene), and it was at that moment in his pocket. He lied therefore most rashly, but with his usual luck.[1]

When Othello 're-enters' the scene, he is the new man we have come to know, a man 'eaten up with passion' for which there is no cause. 'Ha! false to me?' he cries to himself. Nor would he be comforted. 'Avaunt! be gone! thou has set me on the rack' he shouts at his tormentor whose filthy habits of mind and stock of platitudes he has now taken over. In the following lines, where the concept of double-time is said to be at work, Iago's manner of speech has become that of Othello:

[1] *Shakespearean Tragedy* (London, Macmillan, 1957).

> What sense had I of her stolen hours of lust?
> I saw't not, thought it not, it harmed not me:
> I slept the next night well, fed well, was merry;
> I found not carrion kisses on her lips.
> He that is robbed, not wanting what is stolen,
> Let him not know it, and he's not robbed at all.

The last two lines are almost a complete take-over and repeat of Iago's 'reputation' and 'purse' speech behind. They epitomize that complete occupation of Othello's mind and soul by Iago so much commented upon. Othello's epitaph to himself therefore comes in pat:

> I had been happy, if the general camp,
> Pioneers and all, had tasted her sweet body,
> So I had nothing known. O, now for ever
> Farewell the tranquil mind! farewell content!
> Farewell the plumed troops, and the big wars
> That make ambition virtue—O farewell!
> Farewell the neighing steed and the shrill trump,
> The spirit-stirring drum, th' ear-piercing fife
> The royal banner, and all quality,
> Pride, pomp, and circumstance of glorious war!
> And O you mortal engines, whose rude throats
> The immortal Jove's dead clamours counterfeit,
> Farewell! Othello's occupation's gone!

That certainly rises beyond self-dramatization. It is the cry of a man who accepts in the face of all facts that he has lost all. And therein lie our feelings of pity and fear for the man, for as Aristotle again states it for all time 'our pity is awakened by undeserved misfortune, and our fear by that of someone just like ourselves', who neither conspicuous for virtue and justice nor for vice and depravity, falls into misery from one error of judgment arising from his character.

We may in our innocence ask with Iago 'Is't possible?' But for Othello now possessed, it is a matter so urgent that he takes Iago by the throat and goes on to stake his own soul for 'the ocular proof'. In this demand he proves himself the masochist that he really is. 'Be sure thou prove my love a whore' he raves. 'Make me to see 't.' 'Would I were satisfied!' 'Give me a living reason she's disloyal.'

103

Again, Iago can only play it on a low if deep note: 'I see, sir, you are eaten up with passion.' Next, in near desperation, he asks how Othello wants to be satisfied.

> Would you, the supervisor grossly gape on—
> Behold her topped?

'Death and damnation! O!' grunts and gulps the general. Iago, still playing for time to think out some proof, hems and haws:

> It were a tedious difficulty, I think,
> To bring them to that prospect . . .
> It is impossible you should see this,
> Were they as prime as goats, as hot as monkeys,
> As salt as wolves in pride, and fools as gross
> As ignorance made drunk.

'Give me a living reason she's disloyal' Othello insists.

Since for Iago now, it is prove or die, there is in him a new zest to find proof, and as he remarks of himself, he has only to think of a thing evil to 'engender' it there and then. Thus the story of the handkerchief now conveniently to hand and the other, the dream of a Cassio talking of amorous conquests in his sleep.

Othello finds both more than sufficient to take his fatal decision. 'O monstrous! monstrous!' he bellows, bringing out at last the 'savage' in him. 'I'll tear her all to pieces.'

Carried away by such easy success, Iago on his part presses the issue to a point of absurdity not saved this time by the theory of double-time:

> *Iago*:   Tell me but this:
>   Have you not sometimes seen a handkerchief,
>   Sported with strawberries in your wife's hand?
> *Othello*: I gave her such a one; it was my first gift.
> *Iago*:   I know not that; but such a handkerchief—
>   I am sure it was your wife's—did I today
>   See Cassio wipe his beard with.
> *Othello*: If it be that—
> *Iago*:   If it be that, or any that was hers,
>   It speaks against her with the other proofs.

In the desperate game they are in hero and villain forget
that they are still in the one and the same scene where Othello
earlier had put away the handkerchief which Desdemona then
dropped for Emilia to pick up and deliver in triumph to Iago!
In all the frenzy of their act, the savage swears vengeance:

> O, that the slave had forty thousand lives!
> One is too poor, too weak for my revenge.
> *Now do I see 'tis true.* Look: here, Iago,
> All my fond love thus do I blow to heaven—'Tis gone.
> Arise, black vengeance, from thy hollow cell!
> Yield up, O love, thy crown and hearted throne
> To tyrannous hate! Swell bosom, with thy fraught,
> For 'tis of aspics' tongues.

Iago's perfunctory appeal for patience is swept aside with
the demented cry: 'O, blood, blood, blood!' followed by the
fury of a soul more in tumult now than the Pontic sea itself.
The frenzy and fury suddenly become the possession and
esctasy of some dark religion known only to his tribe, as Othello
kneels to take his irrevocable oath:

> Now, by yond marble heaven,
> In the due reverence of a sacred vow
> I here engage my words.

Infected by Othello's passion, Iago too falls on his knees in a
parody of his master's mass:

> Do not rise yet.
> Witness you ever-burning lights above,
> You elements that clip us round above,
> Witness that here Iago doth give up
> The execution of his art, hands, heart
> To wronged Othello's service!

When 'they rise' together both become irrevocably bound to
each other in blood brotherhood, each with his own assign-
ment in their joint mission of sacrifice:

> Within these three days let me hear thee say
> That Cassio's not alive,

enjoins Othello, and promptly Iago answers back:

> My friend is dead:
> Tis done at your request.

As for Desdemona, she will not be cut to pieces any more as previously promised by Othello who now withdraws.

> To furnish me with some swift means of death
> For the fair devil.

'Now art thou my lieutenant' he finally seals the deal, and 'I am your own for ever' Iago returns the grip. And so 'they go'—hand in hand to perdition.

Our argument then is this: in Scene 3 Act 3 is contained all the reversal and discovery that there is in *Othello*, the temptation and fall of the man. Iago has told Othello that Desdemona is Cassio's lover; Othello believes the story, finding proof in the lost handkerchief, and with this confirmation of his wife's unfaithfulness, he swears to take vengeance on her and Cassio with Iago pledging his support. The rest of the action from there should have been plain denouement, that part of the play which Aristotle describes as beginning 'from the onset of the Change to the end'. Milton's Lucifer in *Paradise Regained* tempts Christ three separate times. It will be remembered that that is how it is in the Bible, and it is so because on each occasion Christ successfully resists the Devil. On the other hand, Othello at one attempt falls flat on his face at the feet of Iago, and having fallen, there should be no cause to repeat the act as Shakespeare does again in the first scene of the fourth act.

Here, a brief recapitulation of the superfluous portion of Scene I Act 4 is necessary. It falls into four sections: first, the discussion between Othello and Iago on the innocence or otherwise of love-play and exchange of handkerchief, leading to the fainting-fit of Othello; secondly Cassio's brief intrusion; thirdly, the eavesdropping by a revived but thoroughly shaken Othello upon the interview Iago stages first between himself and Cassio and then between Cassio and Bianca; and fourthly, Othello's fresh desire and decision to murder Desdemona and Cassio. That brings us to line 212, the point at which 'a trumpet sounds' in Lodovico and the scene, we said, ought to have begun.

The discussion, the intrusion, the interviews and eaves-dropping together are part of that other staple of tragedy which Aristotle called complication, namely, 'the part of the story from the beginning to the point immediately preceding the change to good or bad fortune'. And this '... change to ... bad fortune' on the part of Othello is mirrored and evidenced by his precipitate belief in the guilt of his wife, followed by his express desire and decision to murder her and his former lieutenant, all set out above in Scene 3 Act 3.

Now, our case is that Shakespeare represents this crucial turn of events two times over, first in Scene 3 Act 3, as we have seen, and then in Scene 1 Act 4 where the first and fourth sections are actual duplications of that segment of the action which had already been stated elsewhere, namely the un-disputed charge of infidelity made by Iago against Desdemona together with Othello's acceptance of it, followed by his rash vow to avenge himself:

> *Othello*: What dost thou think?
> *Iago*: Think, my lord?

Both lines could well have come from Scene 1 Act 4 which opens with these:

> *Iago*: Will you think so?
> *Othello*: Think so, Iago?

Content, diction, and method in both passages bear so close a similarity that, like Othello himself in the earlier and proper corruption scene, we may be pardoned if the echo disturbs us a bit:

> Think, my lord! Alas, thou echo'st me,
> As if there were some monster in thy thought
> Too hideous to be shown.

And what have the first and fourth sections of Scene 1 Act 4 to show by way of advancing the action of the play or develop-ing its characters? The scene begins with Iago's leading

107

question about kissing in private. 'An unauthorized kiss' asks Othello. Yes, says Iago, adding: 'Or to be naked with her friend in bed / An hour or more, not meaning any harm?' Othello cannot believe this, asking in amazement: 'Naked in bed, Iago, and not mean harm! / It is hypocrisy against the devil.' To which Iago has the prompt reply: 'So they do nothing, 'tis a venial slip'. Once again, Iago, seeing that he can drill his general at will, changes an impersonal situation into a personal one by going yet a third step further: 'But if I give my wife a handkerchief—' 'What then?' Othello starts in his boots. 'Why, then, 'tis hers, my lord; and being hers' / She may, I think, bestow't on any man,' Iago lays down the rule, whereupon Othello feebly appeals for assurance: 'She is protectress of her honour too: / May one give that?' Iago only quickens the pace of the drill: 'Her honour is an essence that's not seen . . . / But for the handkerchief—' That sets Othello jumping and cursing aloud: 'By heaven, I would most gladly have forgot it. / Thou saidst— . . . / he had my handkerchief—' 'Ay, what of that?' Iago warily holds back his hand. 'That's not so good now' Othello admits weakly. Straightaway, Iago takes him on the double march, down a headlong course: 'If I had said that I had seen him do you wrong? / Or heard him say—' Othello who cannot bear it much longer grasps at this: 'Hath he said anything?' Says Iago who can now afford to appear to be holding the other back: 'Faith, that he did—I know not what he did.' But Othello will no longer be stopped. 'What, what?' he shouts. 'Lie' Iago lets the key word be tugged out of him, at which Othello himself wrenches out the damning phrase 'with her'. After that the leash breaks and all vestige of discipline disappears, as the general, let loose by his true lieutenant, goes berserk on the line, 'Lie with her! Lie on her!'

We cannot say that Shakespeare has anything additional to tell us in this opening section of what has been called the other corruption scene except to put on parade once more the corruption of a simple soul through the over-subtle logic of a diabolical mind. That Othello not only grows gibberish but actually 'falls in a trance' under the pressure of Iago's old bag of tricks cannot be due to any new dent made upon a healthy and wholesome frame of mind but purely to the fact that an already derelict and sick person has to behave to a given pattern. 'A horned man's a monster and beast' he cries. It is a part he has accepted and must play. 'Handkerchief—confessions—handkerchief!' he raves on. Next it is 'Pish! Noses, ears, and lips.'

Now, the tragedy suffers if this is merely to show Othello mad, a man devoid of any responsibility for whatever choice or action he may take, Consequently, these cries of his should be taken at best as emanating from a man in the last gasp for breath and who therefore cannot be but incoherent and jerky of rime and reason. But is all this new incident really necessary? Does any of this advance the action of the play, add anything to its overall artistic structure? This 'trance' episode is no more effective as a piece of so-called Senecan sensation than is 'the falling sickness' of Caesar done appropriately enough off-stage in *Julius Caesar.*

The trance, it must be admitted, is induced by a careful manipulation of evidence revealed in four stages: first, the business of kissing in private; secondly, that of being naked in bed with a friend without meaning harm; thirdly, the matter of exchanging handkerchiefs; and fourthly, confessions about the sexual act itself with the play upon the word *lie* echoing the random cue dropped by the Clown behind in Scene 4 Act 3.

Still the question remains: is the incident, from the opening of the scene to line 48, organic to the play? If the excuse is that it provides the proof which Othello wanted of Iago in the first corruption scene, then why present it at this point when the case led by Iago against both Desdemona and Cassio has already been accepted by Othello, and the judgment passed by him one merely awaiting execution? It should be remembered too that these are exhibits and items of proof that at the hearing both prosecutor and judge had agreed were not only impossible but also unnecessary to obtain. Taken as an appeal, a review or retrial of a case already decided by the same court, this section of the scene amounts to simple repetition.

So does that fourth section of this superflous first half of the scene, where 'Cassio goes' after his second entry and interview with Bianca, as Othello who has been eavesdropping 'comes forward' asking: 'How shall I murder him, Iago?' Confused and obviously just recovering from another lapse of memory as confessed by him earlier—

> O, it comes o'er my memory.
> As doth the raven o'er the infected house,
> Boding to all———

Othello forgets he had already decided to murder Cassio (in Scene 3 Act 3) and actually determined the method of execution—at the hands of Iago and within three days. But now in Act 4 Scene 1 he would 'have him nine years a-killing'. In the same fit of fresh justice he restates Desdemona's manner of punishment: 'Let her rot, and perish, and be damned tonight; for she shall not live.' Next he orders: 'Hang her!' and so to his harrowing appeal for sympathy and understanding to the very person he does not know is his tormentor: 'but yet the pity of it, Iago! O Iago, the pity of it, Iago.' For laying bare his breast he gets a deeper thrust of the dagger. 'If you be so fond over her iniquity', taunts Iago, 'give her patent to offend.' And so it is that all the cannibal in the man bursts forth afresh: 'I will chop her into messes'.

In this fury Othello again demands more means of despatching Desdemona: 'Get me some poison, Iago—this night.' Prompt comes the advice: 'Do it not with poison: strangle her in her bed, even the bed she hath contaminated.' 'Good, good: the justice of it pleases; very good' Othello babbles, while for Cassio, as Iago puts it, 'let me be his undertaker'. When the villain adds: 'You shall hear more by midnight', and gets excellent commendation from his commander, we need not wait a moment longer before 'a trumpet sounds' and brings to the scene the one new incident advancing the action of the play—the arrival of Lodovico with directives from Venice which provoke Othello into beating his wife in the open. Beyond this, all that went before was sheer repetition.

The eavesdropping episode should not even have found a place in the plot of *Othello*. As part of the 'complication' material somewhere in the region of Scene 3 Act 3 perhaps, but certainly not where it occurs in the play. Indeed it raises the old business of just how much 'illusion' the dramatist ought to ask of his audience and technique.

> Do but encave yourself,
> And mark the fleers, the gibes, and notable scorns,
> That dwell in every region of his face.

Thus Iago stage-manages Othello in this incident of the play. Again, but for the havoc we accept the villain has since done by his victim, it would be difficult to believe in this process of corruption of Othello's vision through auto-suggestion. There goes a crudity of presentation here that is absent in the earlier incident when Cassio 'goes' hurriedly from Desdemona and Iago suggests to Othello why his disgraced deputy would steal away so guilty-like

> Seeing you coming.

If these excess incidents we have outlined contribute at all to the story of Othello, it is the sensational language as well as the gothic presentation which confounds all illusion. This is a fact painfully confirmed by Sir Laurence Olivier's recent travesty of the part in a production obviously exploiting Joyce Cary's myth of the African from Oxbridge, returning home to his old savage irrational self the moment he is faced with crisis.

From all the above, it is clear that the plot of *Othello* is repetitive of certain incidents representing the action of the play. To cite Aristotle again, a plot's 'various incidents must be so arranged that if any one of them is differently placed or taken away, the effect of the wholeness will be seriously disrupted. For if the presence or absence of something makes no apparent difference, it is no real part of the whole.' Scene 1 Act 4 of *Othello*, from the opening to line 211, can be 'taken away' from the plot, and 'the effect of the wholeness' of the play will *not* be 'disrupted'. Its 'absence . . . makes no apparent difference' to the plot of the play because 'it is no real part of the whole'. Its 'presence' constitutes in fact a repetition of Scene 3 Act 3—the scene central to the play.

Shakespeare then in this respect deviates from the principle guiding the structure of a play in the classical concept of the medium. Perhaps this was what Bradley meant when he said of the play:

> 'In its whole constructional effect *Othello* differs from the other tragedies, and the cause of this difference is not hard to find . . .
> 'I think . . . that the usual scheme is so far followed that the drama represents first the rise of the hero, and then his fall. But . . . one striking peculiarity remains, and is the cause of the unique effect of *Othello*. In the first half of the play the main conflict is merely incubating; then it bursts into life, and goes storming, without intermission or change of direction, to its close. Now, in this peculiarity *Othello* is quite unlike the other tragedies; and in the consequent effect, which is that the second half of the drama is immeasurably more exciting than the first, it is approached only by *Antony and Cleopatra*.'[1]

Far from being 'immeasurably exciting', we find the effect of the play in a particular part of its second half absolutely unbearable. This is because Shakespeare, to draw still on Bradley, has deviated here from his 'usual scheme of an ascending, and a descending movement of one side in the conflict' where the 'general plan is to show one set of forces advancing, in secret or open opposition to the other, to some decisive success, and then driven downward to defeat by the reaction it provokes'.

In abandoning this principle of construction, that of rhythm of tension and relaxation, of rise and fall in tempo of the action so that there is the alternation of disparate passions, all seen in 'the sequence of events within the conflict', by adopting instead the principle of repetition, which enables him to pile on incidents that are identical in content, language and the very emotions they seek to elicit, Shakespeare has constructed a play aspiring to the state and condition of another

[1] Loc. cit.

medium. The form is that of music, and possibly poetry *per se*, each of which can attain intensity simply by repeating motifs, notes, words, lines and even whole passages and tunes. In a play, however, repetition, as Dr Johnson rightly said, far from intensifying, actually dissipates action, dispels belief, tiring eye and mind since the eye, unlike the ear, is less tolerant of illusion which is drama. And this is what happens in *Othello*— a play so beautiful for its 'spectacle, character, . . . diction, song, and thought', we miss its obvious defect of 'plot' as we do with that Odalisque by Auguste Jean Ingres which has thirty-three vertebrae to her voluptuous spine instead of the thirty-two normal with the ugliest of human beings.

Note: All references to Aristotle are taken from the translation of *On the Art of Poetry* by T. S. Dorsch in the Penguin Classics. The edition of *Othello* used is that by Alice Walker and John Dover Wilson for the Syndics of the Cambridge University Press.